GW00708064

SHAFTESBURY

Frontispiece
An aerial view of Shaftesbury from the west. In the left foreground the site of the 'castle' slopes up to the site of the early town and Abbey. Beyond Holy Trinity and its triangle of limes in the churchyard is the close packed street pattern of the medieval town, bounded even now by fields on the east. When this photograph was taken in the 1970's the gasholder, although well concealed from the town, was its most prominent landmark from the air. The new by-pass and Ivy Cross roundabout can be seen at the top of the picture and beyond them fields already beginning to be covered with new houses.

SHAFTESBURY

An Illustrated History

BRENDA INNES

THE DOVECOTE PRESS

Coppice Street in about 1900.

First published in 1992 by The Dovecote Press Ltd.
Stanbridge, Wimborne, Dorset BH21 4JD

ISBN 1 874336 05 9

Brenda Innes 1992

Photoset in Sabon by
The Typesetting Bureau Ltd, Wimborne, Dorset
Origination by Aero Offset Ltd,
Bournemouth, Dorset
Printed and bound in Great Britain by
Biddles Ltd, Guildford and King's Lynn

All rights reserved

Contents

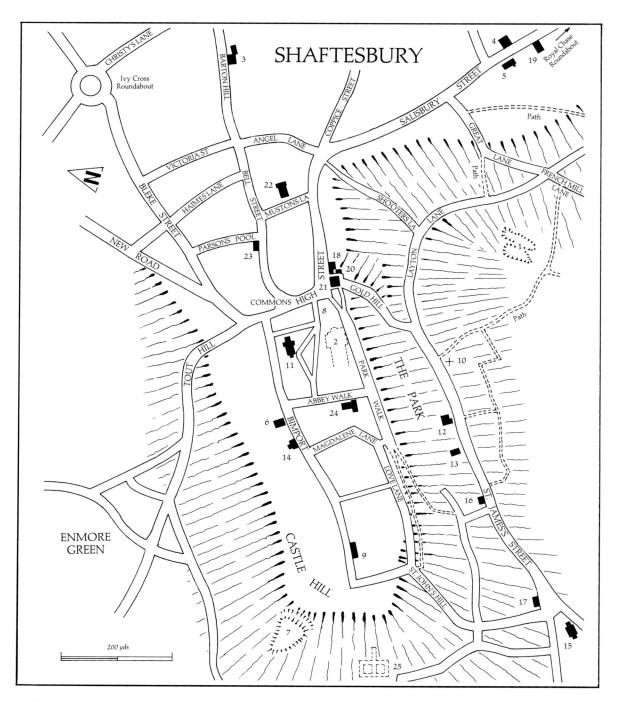

SHAFTESBURY

KEY TO PLAN
1. Abbey Ponds
2. Abbey Ruins
3. Barton Hill House
4. Cann Cottage/Cann Lodge
5. Cann Rectory
6. Castle Hill House
7. Castle
8. Church Lane
9. 'Edwardstowe'
10. Elizabethan House (site of)
11. Holy Trinity Church
12. John Rutter's British School
13. Old Quaker Meeting House
14. Ox House
15. St. James's Church
16. 65 St. James's Street
17. 101 St. James's Street
18. St. Peter's Church
19. St. Rumbold's Church. Cann.
20. Sun and Moon Cottage (Local History Museum)
21. Town Hall
22. United Reform Chapel
23 Wesleyan Methodist Chapel
24. Westminster Memorial Hospital
25. Workhouse (site of)

Introduction

The title of this book could have been: *Shaftesbury: Then as Now* because it became noticeable as I looked into the long history of the town how very much like the present the past has always been. Everyone thinks of Shaftesbury as ancient, but in fact it has no really ancient buildings and few that are even old: what it does have is a continuous history over a period of at least 1,200 years. Kings and queens, great men and women have passed through and it has always attracted visitors, but ordinary people have lived here, enjoying or ignoring the views from their rocky eminence and pursuing ordinary, but interesting, lives.

I would like to introduce people whose writings on Shaftesbury I have quoted. The first is John Hutchins, the vicar who wrote Dorset's great county history, published in 1774. Although he never lived in Shaftesbury Hutchins knew it well as his former tutor at Oxford, John Davys MA, had resigned his living at Castle Ashby in 1742 and retired here, possibly because his family came from Tisbury. John Hutchins records that he 'spent three or four days with him here, and found him as communicative as he was knowing. He carried me over the town, and pointed out all the remains of history, and examined the corporation chest, which contained many curious records relating to the manor, borough, and abbey; and in a subsequent correspondence, supplied me with several valuable materials concerning the ancient and present state of this town'.

A Shaftesbury printer, Thomas Adams, published a history of Shaftesbury in 1807 based heavily on Hutchins. John Rutter, another printer, started to do the same thing in about 1826, but he became so involved in his town that the book was never published. The manuscript for this book, now in the Dorset Record Office, looks nearly complete, he had already run off some trial pages and announced that it was to come out in 1827, but he never printed it.

It was an odd sensation to look at his bundle of papers and handwritten notes, curiously resembling those I was getting together, with incomplete statements ending with a question mark and the note 'check this', adaptations of previous writings about Shaftesbury and notes to remind him to ask various people to ransack their memories for things that had happened before he came to the town. Most surprising of all, many of his opinions, although from a man living in a very different society, seemed to coincide with my own.

John Rutter came to Shaftesbury in 1815 as an apprentice to the Quaker linen draper John Shipley. He was born in Bristol to a reasonably prosperous Quaker family, but was an orphan from the age of ten and brought up by older sisters. He got on well with his

Shaftesbury, described for centuries as 'waterless', actually had its own Mineral Water Works in the nineteenth century. This lemonade bottle boasts 'Shaftesbury water is noted for its purity'.

master, but did not complete his apprenticeship as he inherited some money from his father's will when he was 21, bought a printing press and leased a shop in Shaftesbury High Street to set up as a printer, stationer and bookseller. Only a year later he married Ann Burchett Clarence, the daughter of a woollen draper and upholsterer in the Minories, London, who had been governess to John Shipley's children.

He was young, energetic and obviously not afraid to try any respectable way of earning a living. In 1819 he was advertising a 'newly invented machine, called a Velocipede', priced between 4 and 7 guineas. One was kept in the shop for prospective customers to try, but 'at a reasonable charge', so it is understandable that his business thrived. Between 1822 and 1830 John Rutter was also a publisher. His first publication was a remarkable illustrated book on Fonthill, then probably the most famous house in the country, although hardly the type of house or owner with which one would expect a Quaker publisher to be associated. At this time John Rutter became very much part of the history of Shaftesbury himself, but you must turn to Chapter 5 to find out more about him.

My third 'collaborator' from the past was even more remote from my experience, although nearer in time, as he was a clergyman writing in the 1880's. Charles Mayo had the great advantage of being able to read the original Latin and to examine at leisure in his study the ancient documents relating to Shaftesbury. These were then kept, if not very carefully, in the Town Chest, and many of them have subsequently disappeared. He seems to have been a painstaking and accurate historian and, more surprisingly, wrote a very readable account of his researches which made it a pleasure to use them. I felt a link with him when I found some documents in the Dorset Record Office with the tiny labels neatly tied on by him when he sorted and catalogued the town's untidy collection of deeds over a century ago.

I am also in debt to the founders and members of the Shaftesbury & District Historical Society, who have harvested so much information about the town over the years and to Frank Hopton, a present day member, who has always been available to talk over a knotty point or supply me with information from his fund of knowledge of Shaftesbury and of history in general. The people of Shaftesbury have contributed so much to this book by showing me over their houses, talking of the past and lending photographs to be copied at my long-suffering copy shop (S.O.S.): in particular Marshall Johnson, Dr Tapper, Walter Blake and Mr W. J. Purnell, some of whose photographs appear in the book. Research at my three local record offices (Dorset, Somerset and Wiltshire) the County Libraries of Dorset and Wiltshire, Shaftesbury Library and at the Dorset County Museum has been a real pleasure, and this book would not have been started, let alone finished, without the help and encouragement of my husband Tony.

Saxon Town
880-1065

Signs on the roads leading into Shaftesbury announce it to be a 'Saxon Hilltop Town'. Shaftesbury was certainly a Saxon town and the hilltop, or promontory, is 700 feet above sea level. The site alone makes Shaftesbury unique, but it also has a continuous and interesting history since this early foundation.

Early towns usually grew up where the produce of one area could be traded for that of another having a different type of soil, generally on rivers or the coast because boats were the earliest means of transporting heavy loads. Shaftesbury, however, developed at a meeting point on the dry trackways where the cereals of the chalk uplands could be exchanged for the animal produce of the Blackmore Vale (the chalk and cheese of the old saying). It was also at a point where early travellers going westwards dropped down into the heavy clays, making it a natural halting place. In addition to these factors it was not a bad site for a town as, in spite of what every historian except John Rutter has not realized, the hill on which Shaftesbury is built has a water supply. Unlike the nearby chalk downs it is greensand which, in earlier times when there was a higher water table, would have had springs on the top of the hill as well as those which emerged on the slopes where the greensand meets the clay.

As nearly every high point in the area reveals archaeological evidence of prehistoric settlement it is likely that Shaftesbury's particularly good site would also have been inhabited. However, on this continuously occupied hill any traces of early occupation would be deeply buried and it has not been possible to prove prehistoric settlement from the small-scale excavation feasible when single building sites are examined. In the same way there is no proof of Roman occupation of the site, although there have been a good many Roman 'finds' in the area and there are Roman roads not far away. John Hutchins dismissed the inventive history of a Celtic 'Palador', current when he was writing, with the masterly phrase: 'These fabulous accounts are undoubtedly presumptive of high antiquity, but carry with them no certain information.'

The early English word 'sceaft', meaning the shafts of spears or arrows, may be a reference to the strategic position of Shaftesbury, or to its steep-sided site, and is the word from which the town's name is probably derived. The earliest document thought to refer to Shaftesbury dates from between 670-676 and was a grant to Abbot Bectun of land at Fontmell that was later in the possession of Shaftesbury Abbey. There are also charters given by King Egbert (802-

AELFRED·REX·HA
NC·URBEM·FECIT
ANNO · DOMINIC
AE · INCARNATIO
NIS·DCCCLXXX·
REGNI · SUI · VIII

A rubbing of the lettering on a fragment of stone found on the Abbey site by E. Doran Webb in 1902 (the stone is now lost), and a restored inscription showing how it might have looked when seen by William of Malmesbury (the area included by the rubbing is outlined on the right).

839) and the three older brothers of Alfred, who were all kings of Wessex before him, granting land for a religious purpose, probably a minster or missionary church for people who had settled on the hill and in the surrounding area. These lands are also later found among the property of Shaftesbury Abbey, which has led to the assumption that both a church and a settlement existed before the time of King Alfred.

It cannot be said with certainty that there was no settlement or church here before Alfred founded the Abbey, nor does the date usually given for this foundation appear in any contemporary document. Asser, a Welsh monk who later became Bishop of Sherborne, knew Alfred and described the founding of Shaftesbury Abbey by his King, but he was not concerned with exact dates. A much later monk, William of Malmesbury, writing in about 1125 quoted the inscription on a stone he saw in the Abbey chapter house which recorded the founding of the town in 880 by King Alfred, but a fragment thought to be part of this stone has been dated by its lettering to between 975 and 1050, so it was probably put up more than a century later.

A contemporary document that might have provided an accurate date is the Abbey Charter, but all that survives is a 15th century copy written to form part of a 'cartulary' (a collection of deeds) relating to Abbey properties. As the object of such copies was to defend a monastery from those claiming earlier titles to its land, the age of foundation tends to be exaggerated. Indeed, the copy of Shaftesbury Abbey's charter appears to have such an error as it has as one of its witnesses Eahlfrith, Bishop of Winchester, who is known to have been Bishop there from 871-877, and Alfred did not win the battle for which the Abbey was a thank offering until 878.

This early date also raises problems with regard to Asser's statement that Ethelgiva (Aelthelgeofu), King Alfred's third child or 'midmost' daughter, was the first Abbess, as she was then only a child. She may, of course, have been presented to the new Abbey with the promise that when old enough she would become Abbess, a great honour for the Abbey.

The date of 880 is, however, quite possible in the context of the events of King Alfred's reign. Alfred finally defeated the Danes under Guthrum at the Battle of Edington in Wiltshire in 878, persuaded him and his more important followers to be baptised Christians and to leave Wessex. Alfred had the good sense to realise that after nearly a century of raiding the Danes were unlikely to settle down and become farmers if there was a weak kingdom on their border. To counter this threat he set about reorganizing his country to be always on the defensive, rather like Israel in the 20th century. A document called the 'Burghal Hidage' shows how Alfred's actual defence organization was designed and is now thought to date from very soon after his victory in 878. It lists the 29 'burghs' or manned defence points, plus statistics that enable calculations to be made of the required lengths of their defences and the number of men needed for each one. Shaftesbury was one of these burghs and therefore may well date from 880.

The fact that Shaftesbury's nearest river is more than 5 miles away may have influenced Alfred's decision to found both burgh and nunnery here. He was a shrewd strategist and knew that the seafaring Danes mainly attacked along coasts and up rivers and, while his other fortified towns such as Wareham and Christchurch were placed at points where they could protect Wessex by preventing the raiders from going further up the river routes, Shaftesbury was his ultimate citadel. On this defensible site he placed his Abbey for nuns and in it his daughter who had, according to Asser, 'taken the veil on account of ill health'. The monastery for men he established at the same time was also in the safest place he could find, but Athelney's position amongst impenetrable marshes was obviously not so pleasant or healthy a place as the one he chose for his delicate daughter and her nuns.

In the relatively settled times of the later years of Alfred's reign, and those of his son Edward the Elder, his grandson Athelstan and his great nephew Edgar, Shaftesbury apparently prospered with the rest of Wessex. There is evidence that it was considered to be a reasonably large and important town because in 926 Athelstan decreed that Shaftesbury could have two mints (London had 8, Winchester 6). Manufacturing the coin of the realm was not then an industry that required a large workshop, but owing to its vulnerability to dishonest practice rulers considered it safest for their coin to be made in towns large enough to provide the restraint of public scrutiny, as the moneyer worked in his open fronted workshop; there is a record in a later period that the essential dyes were kept in the church at night.

Asser describes the Abbey as standing by the east gate of the town, suggesting that the earliest town buildings were on the western end of the promontory, with Bimport as a typical spine road. Bimport is an Anglo-Saxon name and was probably the site of the first market: *binan* meaning 'within' and *port* 'market'. It is possible that the earliest Abbey church was of wood, but fragments of Saxon carved stone have been identified from the Abbey ruins indicating a stone building at some time during this period. No foundations have been found, so there is no indication of its plan and the only way any picture can be formed of its possible appearance is by studying the few remaining Saxon churches, such as St. Martin's at Wareham and St. Lawrence's at Bradford-on-Avon. It is just possible that some or all of the earliest houses were also of stone. Although wood is usually the easiest and cheapest material, and was available from the oakwoods growing on the clay lands round Shaftesbury, freestone (i.e. a stone that is easily worked) was even more readily available on the hill itself. The houses would have been simple, single storey buildings, possibly with cellars from which the greensand had been

Saxon carved stones found on the site of the Abbey that bear witness to the presence of a Saxon building.

quarried, with only the Abbey church towering above all else. As Shaftesbury belonged directly to the king, with the Abbess owing allegiance only to him, there is unlikely to have been any lord's mansion or castle in the town.

The Abbey, for its day, would have been an impressive group of buildings, with the Abbey church built with all the skill available, as befitting an offering by the King to God. But housing for the Abbess and nuns, halls for accommodating visitors and buildings for the management of a large farming estate would also have been of a higher than usual standard. The Abbey was of the earliest monastic order, the Benedictine, which was not small and reclusive like many later orders. The Abbess would appear worldly compared to our modern conception of her role: she would have entertained the King and his entourage when in the area and generally taken a vigorous part in the life of the kingdom, as she came from royal or upper class stock her social position was already established.

It is likely that Shaftesbury's original Abbey and town were all to the west of a defensive wall or bank, which completed the protection provided by a simple palisade on the steep slope on the other three sides. No firm evidence of these defences has been found on any of the lines projected on the Burghal Hidage wall length calculation of 2,888 feet. If this measurement is taken round the top of the modern steep slope, roughly along the line of Bimport, St. John's Hill, Love Lane, it would appear that either the early Abbey stood further to the west than the one whose foundations remain or was outside the town defenses. It was, after all, described as being to the east of the town, in which case the Abbey church itself may have been a defensive building and part of the wall, like the church at the tiny Burghal Hidage burgh of Lyng in Somerset.

The absence of any trace of these defences may be simply due to the constant re-use of this land over 1,200 years, but even by the reign of Alfred's grandson Athelstan (925-939) changes were being made in the Burghal Hidage towns. Some were abandoned, others moved to more habitable sites and others, probably including Shaftesbury, were refortified, either as Athelstan proceeded to extend his kingdom or in the less happy times of Ethelred II – when the defences were needed again.

As Shaftesbury continued to be an important place, a new line of defences may have been built where the 14th century wall now stands on Gold Hill, across what is now the Commons and down the west side of Tout Hill. There would have been at least one gate, probably at the end of Bimport. Another development of the town that may have taken place between 900 and 1035 was expansion outside the east wall: pottery thought to date from this period was found in a large pit under the 16th century crypt of St. Peter's church.

Athelstan did not marry and the throne descended to Alfred's other grandsons Edmund and Eadred and to his great grandson Edgar.

The royal connection with Shaftesbury continued and King Edmund's widow St. Elgiva (Aelfgifu) became a nun and was buried here. Unfortunately, King Edgar married twice and his second queen reputedly murdered his heir King Edward in 979, leading to the succession of her son as Ethelred II, a king who seems to have earned his soubriquet of 'unready' or unwise. The result was that the years of prosperity ended as Wessex once again faced attacks from the Danes. Shaftesbury, however, benefited greatly from this murder as the burial place of the martyred king.

There was nothing saintly about Edward's brief life or his death

Part of an alabaster altar piece which probably came from the Abbey. It is of a type made near Nottingham before 1400. It probably represents the translation (re-burial) of St. Edward the Martyr in the Abbey. Having been walled up for centuries it retains traces of its bright colours, unlike similar alabaster carvings set into the four sides of a cross now in the Abbey grounds which are badly weathered.

13

Shaftesbury on its 'promontory' from the south: the view that would have greeted the procession bringing the martyred King Edward's body up from Wareham. Holy Trinity church in the centre of the picture is near the site of the Abbey church and its tower is probably of the same height. No evidence has been found for houses on Gold Hill, seen winding up to St. Peter's on the right, before about 1200, but this may have been the route up to the town and Abbey even in the Saxon period.

at the hands of his step-mother's servants while on a hunting expedition in Purbeck, but anointed kings were specially venerated at this time and, while his assassins made frantic efforts to dispose of his body, people began to report miracles in connection with it. It will never be known whether the Abbess of Shaftesbury proceeded 'with an eye to business' after hearing about these miracles, or for some more laudable reason obtained the burial of King Edward at her Abbey, but the body was brought with great ceremony from Wareham where it had received temporary burial. Having St. Edward's shrine was of benefit to her Abbey to the end of its days, and to Shaftesbury possibly even longer. Pilgrims travelled long distances to the tomb, more miracles were reported and more pilgrims came, bringing offerings to the Abbey and trade to the town. The dedication of the Abbey was amended to St. Mary & St. Edward and Shaftesbury was sometimes called Edwardstowe. Strange, but no stranger than coach loads of tourists coming to see the street where an advertisement was made!

The dating to between 975-1050 of the stone attributing the foundation of Shaftesbury to King Alfred puts it squarely into Ethelred II's reign of 976-1015, and the Royal Commission for Historic Monuments consider this stone was originally set in a defensive gateway. It seems likely that Ethelred would build defences for his brother's shrine and be anxious to emphasise his descent from his famous ancestor King Alfred to distance himself from his more immediate forbears. However, the theory that Ethelred built a defensive wall at Shaftesbury appears to be contradicted by his grant of

14

the monastery at Bradford-on-Avon to the Shaftesbury nuns as a place to which they could take his brother's remains and find sanctuary from the Danes. This is one interpretation of Ethelred's grant, the other is the exact opposite, that Shaftesbury was the refuge. Historians are divided on this interpretation, but on a comparison of the two sites Shaftesbury seems to be the safer place as Bradford was on the navigable Avon, nearer to the coast and was in fact sacked by the Danes in 1015. There is also the possibility in a long reign like Ethelred's, that Shaftesbury was at first considered defendable but later regarded as a poor defensive risk, particularly when the Danes began to settle.

In 1941 the 'Shaftesbury Hoard' was unearthed just outside the town; the 100 or so silver coins of King Ethelred II had probably been buried in a similarly unsettled time. There were coins from 54 different moneyers in 21 towns, more than half from York and Lincoln and only one from Shaftesbury, which had been in a metal bound wood or leather box. The site was subsequently cleared for road building so archaeologists cannot now discover whether they were buried under a house or in the open. They could have been buried by a Shastonian in fear of the Danish raiders who were in Dorset in 998 and 1003, or even by a terrified Danish settler as he fled from the massacre of Danes ordered by Ethelred in 1002 on St. Brice's Day. Alternatively they could have been buried by someone afraid to enter the town carrying a large amount of money, who for some reason never returned.

Although the Danes raided along the coast and well inland in Dorset there is no record of Shaftesbury being a victim of their attacks during the reign of Ethelred or his son Edmund. In 1017, after defeating Edmund, the Danish Canute became King of England and in 1035 died as an honoured guest, a patron and probably a patient of the nuns at Shaftesbury, although he was buried in the royal place of interment at Winchester.

A typical coin of Ethelred II, one of nearly 100 found in the Shaftesbury Hoard. These were made by hammering a silver 'blank' between the dies issued, and strictly controlled, by the King.

Medieval Shaftesbury
1066-1539

A fragment of a medieval corbel excavated from the Abbey.

William the Conqueror appears to have entertained kindly feelings towards Shaftesbury Abbey, restoring the manors of Cheselborne and Stour that had been appropriated by Harold and, when he wanted Abbey land to build Corfe Castle, allowing the Abbess the valuable church of Gillingham in exchange. Nor did William interfere with the dedication of the Abbey, although elsewhere worship of Saxon saints was forbidden. Perhaps he found veneration of St. Edward expedient, as one of his claims to the English throne was his own rather remote relationship to Edward's line.

The Domesday Book compared the year it was made (1086) with the time of Edward the Confessor and reveals pre-conquest Shaftesbury as the largest of the four Dorset boroughs, with three moneyers and 257 houses. By 1086 there were only 177 houses, possibly it suffered by being on the line of march when William crossed Dorset on his way to subdue Exeter in 1068 or when troops were sent from Winchester to quell a rising at Montacute the following year.

William of Malmesbury in 1125 described Shaftesbury as 'a town no longer only a village', however the Abbey church was being rebuilt at this time, with the typical Norman round ended chancel and chapels. The nuns had direct connections with the Church in Normandy, where the names of Shaftesbury's abbesses have been found on a Bede Roll (a list of people for whom prayers are to be said).

It seems likely that the houses that disappeared between 1066-1086 were part of the Saxon town in the Bimport area and that these were not rebuilt. perhaps because the Abbey needed more space. It does not seem to have been because a castle was imposed on the town, as happened in other places: the earthworks always known as the Castle are now thought to have been the remains of one built during the civil wars at the time of King Stephen (1135-54). The most likely reason for the shift of the town centre eastwards is that the Abbey had established a market place outside the town wall and when the town began to prosper again traders (merchants is perhaps too grand a term for Shaftesbury), built their combined houses, stores and workshops around the market. The parish churches of St. Peter, St. James and St. Rumbold, together with those that later disappeared, St. Lawrence and St. Martin, probably originated about 1200. Holy Trinity may have been built to remove the necessity of allowing townspeople into the nuns' church. It was first mentioned in 1364 when a priest was transferred there from the Abbey and Hutchins only lists its rectors from 1414.

Meanwhile an 'industrial suburb' may have been beginning to develop down in St. James, where there was sun and shelter for orchards, or even vineyards and a spring line providing copious water for trades like tanning and cloth processing. Springs were also used to fill artificial clay-lined ponds to rear the 'carpes and tenches' essential for Fridays and other fast days in the Abbey. Further down the slope where the springs became vigorous, little streams fed the water mills that served the Abbey and town, probably on the sites of Gear's and French Mills. A large piece of land, some of it in St. James, has the Roman sounding name Liberty of Alcester, but was given by its Norman overlord in about 1140 to a monastery he was founding at Alcester, near Birmingham.

By the time there is documentary evidence of the eastward expansion of Shaftesbury it had become the 'city' with 12 churches, abbey and mints that writers have romanticised. City it was not, but it was considered to be a town by the Crown, which gradually extended its privileges. In 1252 Henry III ordered that his travelling judges should visit Shaftesbury, a privilege which also brought business to the town. From about 1295 Shaftesbury also had two members representing it in Parliament, a considerable expense as they received two shillings for each day spent at the King's court, but obviously of value to the town. Shaftesbury had not yet acquired the privilege of a mayor and corporation.

The main feature that distinguished a town in the Middle Ages was the right to hold markets and fairs, which had been granted to the Abbey very early on. Shaftesbury was well positioned for the exchange of commodities and perhaps the fact that the town can be seen from as much as ten miles away in most directions acted in its favour. Market towns in southern England tend to be 10-20 miles apart and the factor that probably weighed heaviest in deciding to which market a person would go, apart from distance, was where they thought they would make the best sale or purchase. It was therefore vital for a market to attract as large a number of people as possible and to establish a reputation for fair dealing. The market brought in, not only the rents, but also fees for measuring and weighing goods being sold. There were also special rapid justice courts at the fairs from which the penalties went to the markets' proprietor. These had the Norman-French name of *pied poudre*, meaning dusty feet, cheerfully anglicised by the ordinary folk at the receiving end as 'courts of pie powder'.

The only archaeological survivals that Shaftesbury has from before about 1200 are the foundations of the abbey church, probably the town's present street pattern and the base of a pillar from an earlier church, visible through a special viewing window in St. Peter's Church floor. Other buildings were probably of stone, and the constant quarrying away of the town site probably means that the ground levels and slopes visible today are not the ones that would have existed at earlier times in the town's history. While quarrying

Until quarrying ceased in the late 19th century Shastonians were aware of the Greensand rock underneath them and referred to the town as 'the rock'. The bedrock from which the 14th century Abbey wall springs is one of the few remaining places where it can now be seen.

would have produced some of the unnaturally steep slopes and cliffs that still exist around the town the usual reaction to a hole, to tip rubbish into it, would have further altered the contours of Shaftesbury.

In the Middle Ages the country was ruled directly by kings whose court moved around in order that it did not exhaust the food supply in any one place. They kept in touch with other parts of the realm by means of an efficient system of royal couriers and the documents carried were carefully preserved as they formed the basis of the law. From some of these surviving requests and orders a vivid picture of life in Shaftesbury can be obtained.

An order in 1275 to Adam de Wintoria (Adam of Winchester) commands him to buy 30 tuns of wine for the King, 15 of which are to be sent to Gillingham against the King's arrival. On November 11 the Sheriff of Dorset was ordered to send 30 quarters of wheat to Shaftesbury to be there eight days before Christmas: it looks as if Edward I was planning to spend the Christmas of 1275 in Shaftesbury. Not only did Kings stay at the Abbey, they also used it as a prison for female diplomatic prisoners and a retirement home for royal servants.

In 1312 a safe conduct was issued for the King's Commissioners to bring Elizabeth, wife of Robert the Bruce of Scotland, and Margery her step-daughter to Shaftesbury as prisoners. The safe conduct was neccessary because as the wife of the King's enemy she would, if not under his protection, have been outside the law. If the Abbess had allowed Elizabeth to escape she would have been heavily fined, as in fact the Abbess was in 1291 when she was ordered to pay the King 100s for the flight of a criminal. Sibyl Libaud also came from Scotland, but was more of a religious refugee than a prisoner, at least if we take this request at its face value: 'The King sends Sibyl Libaud of Scotland who lately came to England to the King's faith and besought that he would provide for her maintenance . . . to provide her and her son Thomas, who is of tender age, with . . . food and clothing until Whitsuntide next' (from December) 'knowing that what they do at his request shall not be to the prejudice of her house in future'. This last remark emphasises the importance attached to precedents.

In the reigns of Edward I and II a series of pensioners were sent to the Abbey, including Henry Bishop, the King's Yeoman and Richard Knyght 'spigurnel of the Kings chancery who has long served the King and his father in that office'. Some royal pensioners collected their pensions directly from money owed to the King by the Abbey or the town. In 1376 the Abbess was told to pay King Richard II's physician, Master John Bray, a pension of 12 marks a year. The following year his wife Joan is to 'receive such maintenance as Juliana Spencer deceased had by the command of the King', but Joan was not a widow retiring to the Abbey, as a later grant in the Patent Rolls of 1378 confirms that John Bray has been retained by Henry IV. Another highly regarded royal servant was Joan Gambon, a 'damsel of Isabella, the King's daughter', presumably a lady-in-waiting as she was granted an extra 40s pension for her 'long service to Queen Philippa', Isabella's mother, 'to be received of the issues of the toll of that town', which the bailiffs of Shaftesbury in 1339 appear to have been somewhat tardy in producing.

The traffic was not entirely one way: timber from the royal forest of Gillingham was given to Shaftesbury Abbey in 1275. Possibly the twenty oaks were used to roof the substantial nave with its sturdy round stone pillars that is thought to have been built at that time to

An illuminated illustration showing 'The Three Marys at the Sepulchre' from a beautiful prayer book or psalter made between 1130 and 1140 to be used in the great Norman Abbey church. It was made in the West Country specifically for the nuns at Shaftesbury, possibly by the nuns themselves.

accommodate the increasing number of pilgrims who came to worship at King Edward's shrine. Money was also given by Kings to the Abbey: the Abbess's duty of providing three knights to fight for the King had evidently been exchanged for a payment, but Edward I, from court at Stourton, reduced this by 30 marks 'of his grace' and this was further reduced by 20 marks 'at the instance of Alphonse his son'. At this period also Queen Eleanor owed the Abbess 50 marks.

Abbesses and Queens may have been friendly, but perhaps there was rivalry among their servants in 1340. For more than a century, since Count John of Mortain had given his 'dearest friend Abbess Mary' four horse loads of brushwood a day (except Sundays) from the Royal Forest of Gillingham, this important fuel for cooking and heating had been free to the Abbey. However an enthusiastic 'new broom', Geoffrey de Coles, sent down to survey the manor and forest for Queen Philippa, did not know this and ordered the foresters to unload the Abbess's pack horses and not to send any more wood up to the Abbey.

Shaftesbury Abbey was so popular that there were frequent commands to the Abbess to reduce the number of nuns admitted. The first on record was from the Pope in 1218 who decided that 100 was the limit above which they would not be able to support themselves and give alms to the poor.

Shaftesbury Abbey's original foundation had given it extensive lands and nuns from local families had endowed it with more, which meant that there was little land left to endow new foundations. One of the nearest was a nunnery at Tarrant Crawford founded by Bishop Richard Poore (1217-29), who also wrote a book of advice for his nuns that was as practical as his transfer of his cathedral from the cramped hill of Old Sarum to the spacious, well-watered meadows of Salisbury. Bishop Poore was also adviser to the Abbess and nuns of Shaftesbury and perhaps his experience with them inspired some of what he wrote in his 'Ancren Riwle'. He recommends nuns not to be too austere, they can have a pet cat, but cautions against luxuries such as gloves and exotic pets.

Relations between the great Benedictine Abbey and the smaller Cistercian house seem to have been amicable: in 1278 the Abbess of Tarrant requested the King to restore land at Gussage St. Andrew to Shaftesbury Abbey. Dealings with nuns who followed a similar rule were good, but an order from King Henry II in 1256 reveals Shaftesbury Abbey in the role of oppressor encroaching on the land of the ultra austere Carthusian monks at Witham Priory, who rarely left their cells and 'cannot and will not plead to recover their rights in any secular court'. The lives of these monks contrast stongly with Shaftesbury's nuns, five of whom were to be provided with 'a horsed vehicle for their journey both ways' when they went to confer with the Archbishop of York at the request of Henry III.

Some novices must have been happy to go into the Abbey but others, perhaps placed there by families anxious to protect the

family honour, must have found it repressive. Their frustration may have produced the tough abbesses who disputed financial and other rights with their Kings and usually won. In 1293 the Abbess obtained the right of free warren in seven of her manors: one, La Bertone, included Wincombe Park where the house of the 'Warrenario' is recorded after 1539. Rabbits were only introduced about 1275 and considered a Royal delicacy. A less Abbess-like demand was for the right to sea wreck. Shaftesbury Abbey owned the manor of Kingston on Purbeck whose dangerous shore was on the then heavily-used sea route between Normandy and Wareham. In the 1260's Luke de Tany, Constable of Corfe Castle, had claimed this right, but in 1270 Henry III restored to the 'Abbess and her successors the whole wreck at sea in their said manor without impediment'. Another valuable product that the Abbey obtained from its property on Purbeck was salt, then essential for preserving food. The Abbey owned the village of Arne where more than 20 tenants worked salt pans; their dues to the Abbey being paid both in agricultural work and in salt making. Other tenants from as far away as Fontmell Abbas had, as part of their obligation to the Abbey, the job of carrying salt from Arne, also herrings from Wareham, which were probably packed in salt to preserve them.

The abbesses were spirited in the defence of their house, but the nunnery appears to have been generally well conducted, although the Abbess was warned in 1309 not to allow her nuns to go into the town 'lest scandal enter in'. Other criticisms often quoted are the 'Abbess's' failure to repair the stocks or clear rubbish from the King's Highway, but these are the failures of her male servants. The Abbey was in constant financial difficulties in spite of the wealth implied by the oft quoted, but exaggerated, saying that 'If the abbot of Glastonbury might marry the abbess of Shaftesbury, their heir

Place Farm, Tisbury. Part of the wide possessions of Shaftesbury Abbey, this was a 'grange' from which the Abbey estates in the area were managed by the Abbess's stewards. The huge tithe barn was used to store grain before threshing. With a similar magnificent barn at Bradford on Avon these are the only remaining buildings of Shaftesbury Abbey.

would have more land than the King of England'.

It is probable that by 1348 England had reached a point where the population was too great for the food produced. Several wet summers reduced cereal crops while damp induced disease among the sheep, which were depended upon for their milk and meat as well as their profitable wool, causing most of the population to be weakened by under-nourishment. War also seems to have played its usual part in the disaster that followed, for King Edward III's victorious army from Crecy and Calais came back to England carrying the disease that was already decimating Europe. Many accounts trace the beginning of the Black Death in Britain to one ship arriving at Weymouth, but its source and the real numbers of people it killed are as impossible to define as what the disease actually was.

No record exists of the number of nuns that died as a result of the Black Death, but no further complaints are recorded of there being too many of them. The difficulties of running the Abbey increased with the shortage of workmen and the Abbess was still having problems 30 years after the first wave of the disease when her 'bondmen in Bradford, Co. Wilts refused their services'. Similarly no record exists of the number of townspeople who died, but in four out of eight parishes the incumbent died in 1348 and in three others he may have done, which, even allowing for the additional risk a priest would run, is a dreadful toll.

In such circumstances it is not surprising to find a preoccupation with death, and it is a will that gives the first real insight into everyday life in the town. Alice atte Hall made her will in autumn 1348 just after St. Peter's church, to which she left some money, had instituted its third rector in a year. She also left money to three cathedrals: Salisbury, Wells and Chichester, but nothing to the Abbey or Holy Trinity church, although she was to be 'well and honourably buried' in its churchyard and lived in the parish. Her next door neighbour was Peter Selwood, a leading figure in the town and one of her executors was Nicholas Harding, a member of another prominent family, so she was probably well off, but specific items she left look modest by modern standards. Her son Robert got the best bed and the 'best brazen pot' and that was apparently all he did get. Richard Goche got the third best bed and second best pot, but her executors were to sell her tenement and 'pay thence to Richard Goche'. Whether this was a debt or whether he was to arrange for the masses is not clear, her will only says 'All that remains of the proceeds to be distributed in Masses and in bread among the poor of Shaston, for my soul.' By contrast the will of Isabella Hulling who died in 1442 appears to be the will of a younger woman with her thoughts less on religious things: she left money to her parish church and Salisbury cathedral, but also remembers her cousin Margaret who is to have 'my best gown' and Isabella Obus who gets 'one red petticoat'.

Alice atte Hall was making provision for her soul in a way that was fairly new at the time. The previous practise had been to bequeath property and leave the church to administer it, which resulted in a steady shift of land to religious houses. Kings did not regard this with total approval, sometimes seeing the clergy more as temporal rivals than spiritual guides. Nevertheless in 1318 the Abbey was allowed to accept the rent from a property in Donhead from Stephen Pruet, the parson of Compton, to pay for 'a light to burn through the whole of the night in the cloister of the Abbey'. At least five other gifts of property to pay for daily services were allowed before 1340, so with the frequent devotions of the nuns and prayers offered by pilgrims the Abbey church would have been a busy place.

Among the documents catalogued by Charles Mayo in 1887 were many 'Charters of Feoffment'. These were for properties managed by a group of feoffees or trustees who used the rents to pay for church services, called 'Obits' or 'Placebos', for the souls of the donors and their relations. The trustees were usually the town's leading men, whilst the witnesses to the deeds were headed by the mayor. This fact enabled Mayo to triumphantly produce the names and dates of 27 mayors Hutchins had not discovered, including one from 2 years earlier than the first his predecessor had listed, so that he could demonstrate that, although there is no record of the institution of the position of mayor in Shaftesbury, John de Haselmere was mayor in 1352.

The detailed locations described in these deeds, necessary in the days long before street numbering, give street names and in a few cases indicate where people lived more than 500 years ago. John and Joane Kilpeke probably did not live in the house they left to pay for an obit in St. Peter's church for themselves and his parents, Robert and Alice Kilpeke, as John was a goldsmith in Bristol. The property was described as being on Gold Hill and Mayo traced the ownership back to a Robert Culpek before 1429, who he concluded was Robert Kilpeke's father (spelling of a name can vary in the same sentence in early documents). The Kilpeke's house was between St. Peter's church and another tenement, therefore probably where Sun & Moon Cottage is today. Mayo also found a description of a hall-type house on this site in 1360. We know it was fairly large, with a hall and central open hearth, because Nicholas Thomere, who was leasing it to Henry and Alice Hastiler, 'reserved to his own use one upper chamber on the south part of the hall, and a stable, for himself and his horse, with free ingress and egress, at convenient times, whensoever he would.'

Another property used to endow an obit can be identified as standing where St. Peter's church hall is today, because someone had later written on the deeds 'Conveyance of the Lamb'. But it was not an inn when William Ketylton, rector of the combined churches of St. Peter and St. Martin, acquired 'two messuages with solers, sellers, gardynes and courtelages thereto belonging' from 'Robert Lawrence,

The beautiful vault of the 'new' porch added to St. Peter's church in the Tudor period, note the Tudor rose in the centre, possibly at the time of Henry VII's visit in 1491. The stone used is not the local greensand, but a more easily carved limestone which would probably have originally been coloured and gilded.

citizen and draper of London and Margaret his wife' in 1504.

It appears that in late medieval Shaftesbury Gold Hill was a good address, particularly the top which formed the east side of the market place that contained the fish cross, with the growing splendour of St. Peter's church at the corner where it joined the Cornmarket (now the High Street). St. Peter's was apparently rebuilt between 1400 and 1500. The interior would have been a blaze of light and colour with enlarged windows containing stained glass, chantry altars, images of saints and bishops, all brightly painted and gilded, with candles and oil lamps burning before them. St. Peter's still possesses the ends of some of the first benches made for the church (previously worshippers had stood or knelt on the rush-strewn floor).

Although there were always those who preferred drinking and playing games to actually attending services, the parish churches of medieval Shaftesbury would have been familiar to everyone, as they were used for all sorts of meetings and entertainments. In Shaftesbury the buildings and their abundant decoration were paid for by ordinary people rather than by one or two rich merchants, as was the case in many other places. A list of Shaftesbury taxpayers in 1340 contains a greater number of names than any other Dorset town, but none were paying the highest amount.

The much publicised decay of Shaftesbury's Medieval churches can be accounted for by the fact that many had little or no land to produce tithes for their support and tended to fade out when waves of religious fervour subsided, leaving abandoned buildings which either fell down or were used for other purposes, rather like non-conformist chapels today. The survivors, in particular St. Peter's and St. James, which had both had other parishes added to them by 1500, seem to have been well supported by their parishioners and by their church guilds. Church guilds enabled less wealthy people to have prayers said for their souls and, in addition to organizing these religious services and paying chaplains, the guilds provided much of the social life in the Middle Ages, with processions and fund raising activities such as church ales. Cakes and specially brewed ale were sold to raise money for the church: a more robust form of coffee morning. A large fireplace under the south aisle of St. Peter's (now the doorway of a cloakroom) may be where the ale was brewed.

The only suggestion of a medieval trade guild in Shaftesbury lies in the record of a building at the top of Gold Hill called the 'Gild

These niches are the remains of chantry altars where special masses were said by chantry priests to speed the souls of the recently dead through purgatory. Traces of their original bright colouring can be seen after being covered with whitewash for several centuries.

Hall' in 1496, but this was the name given to the Town Hall where courts were held and the mayor and other officials appointed. This could be the origin of the name of the hill, but I have found no earlier reference to Gild Hill, while Gold Hill or Goldhulle occurs as far back as 1350. The lists of trustees sometimes give occupations and include all the ones that would be expected in a market town, such as butcher, baker, carpenter and tanner. Surnames cannot be regarded as an indication of occupation at this late date, but there are two in the 1340 list of taxpayers that would have been originally given to stonemasons, a trade that must have been carried on here since the town began. No trade seems to have been dominant and it is doubtful if Shaftesbury was large enough to have a guild for any single trade.

Towards the end of the medieval period it is noticeable that 'wevers' and mercers begin to appear frequently among the leading citizens. While Shaftesbury never became famous as a clothmaking town, wool cloth must have been the town's only product that was made for export, and not merely concerned with its main role of being a market for the surrounding area. In 1458 one of the mills at Cann was being used for fulling cloth, it was leased by John Shoil who was described as a mercer. A number of other mercers are listed at this time and one as a mercer on one document and a weaver on another. This suggests that a mercer was not a shopkeeper who sold cloth, but the local name for what were called 'clothiers' in the main cloth producing districts further north. There, being a weaver was the usual first step towards joining the ranks of those who bought raw wool, had it cleaned and spun (usually by women), put it out again to be woven by weavers working in their own homes and took it back to be fulled in their mills. It is unlikely that it would have been dyed here because the white English broadcloth was usually finished abroad, although the mud-free chalk streams around Shaftesbury would have provided suitable water.

What might be described as Shaftesbury's major industry was obviously well established by the end of the Middle Ages. Although the Abbey entertained the highest and the lowest, Royal visitors and penniless travellers, there appear to have been enough paying customers to make innkeeping a trade which could bring a Shastonian to the front rank of citizenry, as one or two of the town council are so described. Inns of which there is a written record include the 'Bell', which gave its name to Bell Street, the 'Ram' just round the corner in Bleke or Ram Street, and the 'Swan' which was possibly the inn held by John Croxhale in 1428, as it was on the north side of the High Street where his inn was said to be. The 'George' and the 'Angel' were popular names for medieval inns, but there is no documentary evidence of these inns in Shaftesbury before 1539, although they are recorded shortly afterwards.

For travellers, able to afford the board but not the bed, there were the alehouses for which Shaftesbury was famous. At one court in

A drawing, apparently of a carved stone that adorned the old 'Bell' inn.

26

1471 no less than seventeen of them were fined for selling ale in 'cups' which were not of the standard measure. As the job of enforcing the laws for weights and measures, also collecting the fines, was highly sought after it was obvious that this was no isolated occasion. Even the ecclesiastical alemakers were not spared: in 1480 the Wardens of the Goods of St. Peter's church, the Wardens of the Fraternity of St. Gregory and the Wardens of the Goods of St. Clements, groups one would suppose of exemplary citizens, were all fined for the same offence.

In spite of the amount of ale that evidently flowed in Shaftesbury it did not apparently have a reputation as a particularly violent place. It is difficult to get a true picture when few records survive. The royal forests around Shaftesbury tend to unbalance the view further as trespasses of vert and venison, such as William Anketil was pardoned for in 1310, were not anything we should take too seriously today. It is possible that the harsh forest laws made criminals and that the woodland attracted outlaws. In the 1340's there were enquiries into 'illicit meetings in Gillingham and Shaftesbury by warlike men' who had been 'extorting money by threats, robbery, breaking houses and taking goods to no small value'. Two groups of men had already been ordered to investigate, but seem to have failed as there were complaints by 'the Abbess and the King's men and tenants in the town of Shaftesbury' that 'there has as yet been no remedy applied'.

The silver gilt arms plate of Shaftesbury's older mace. It is engraved with 'per fess France and England' on the left, the arms of the Abbey in the centre indicating that it was made before the Dissolution and 'a lion rampant beside a tree', on the right. It has been carried before Shaftesbury's mayors for upwards of 400 years.

Excavations at the Abbey have so far revealed only parts of the nuns church, with the cloister and chapter house on the south, but a schedule of 1565, quoted by Hutchins, lists over 40 major 'chambers' and as many ancillary buildings. Among the enclosed accommodation for the nuns it lists the 'mynchen' (nuns) chamber, perhaps the parlour where the rule of silence was relaxed and the nuns spent their free time; the 'Utter Nurcery', possibly for the novices; and the wardrobe chamber where robes and Abbey linen were made and repaired. Possibly the 'faire lodging', the 'Greene Chamber' and 'Starre Chamber' were the Abbess' accommodation. The 'covent kitchen' where the nuns food, curiously like a present day health conscious diet with no red meat, was prepared and the 'frayt' or nuns dining room.

There was another kitchen in which food for visitors was prepared by lay men and women. Some idea of the importance of a job in this kitchen can be gained from an inheritance described in 1329. Roger de Melbury or Roger le Couk of Melebury had died and his son William who was 14 and a ward of King Edward III was to inherit not only land, but a 'corrody' or 'provision for maintenance', 'to be received in the abbey viz a loaf called 'Koytlouf', a gallon of ale and a dish from the kitchen everyday, for which corrody he ought to be cook in the kitchen of the Abbess, to take the accustomed fee and to take charge of all the copper, silver and brazen vessels in the said

One of the inlaid medieval tiles that covered the floor of the Abbey church, probably made locally. Heraldic designs were cut into a leather hard tile and the cut away portions filled with 'slip' or liquid clay. When partly dried the surplus was scraped from the surface of the tile to leave the sharp edged cream pattern on the red tile, which was then glazed and fired.

The head of a Tudor figure found in the Abbey ruins.

kitchen'. It sounds as if William le Couk would be quite an important person when he took up his inheritance. I hope some of the 8 pints of ale in his 'cooks perks' went to quench the thirst of the minions he must have employed.

This kitchen served the 'broad hall with its buttery and pantry at the north end' where kings and other important visitors would have dined. Beneath it were extensive 'sellers', some specifically for wine, and 'thalmery' (the almery) where food and clothes were issued to the poor. Considerable quantities were involved and the Abbey was self supporting with the 'great bakehouse' and its 'pastryhouse', 'bredhouse' with a hearth house and a 'chamber' for the baker. The Abbey also produced that other essential of medieval life: ale, with malthouse, brewhouse with its 'fyer house' and the 'maltsmen's chamber'. A team of workers would have brewed continuously to supply the quantities needed.

There was a 'hoopers house' where casks were made, not only for ale, but also to store dry foods in safety; the 'grynter' house or granary was placed on an upper floor to make it easier to keep out rats and mice. The wool house underneath it also needed protection, for wool was the Abbey's main source of income, as can be deduced from the alternate demands for money and wool by kings in search of the means of waging war. In 1346 and 1347 thirty sacks of wool were loaned to Edward III for his war with France and a promise by the same King in 1340 prices wool at 100s a sack.

The outer parts of the Abbey included 'The cheker, and the chamber next unto it, called the Cheker Chamber, with the entry into the same, where the court hath been allweys kept for the King'. The steward, the most important layman in the Abbey who officiated at the Abbess's courts, had his 'chamber with a study and loft over' nearby. These and some other buildings probably formed part of the main gate of the Abbey, but no trace remains of what was usually an impressive building.

Another unsolved mystery is the site of the well or wells. The 1565 division of the property into three allocates a third of the well and laundry house to each part, underlining its importance to a tenant and suggesting that there was only one well. Whether this was on the top of the hill, where Laura Sydenham in her plan of the Abbey shows a well discovered in 1938 and several wells of undetermined age have been found, or in Laundry Lane is difficult to say. Other mysteries are the 'lyme house', which may have been where limewash was prepared for the walls, and the 'longe leden chamber'. Important buildings were usually lead roofed, but the old English word 'leden' meant Latin or language, so it may have been a school: there is a reference to an obit for a schoolmaster at the Abbey.

From the early 1400's there were stirrings of discontent with the religion that had been so long practised. These came mainly from practical working men who scorned images, pilgrimages and the influence of a foreign pope. They wished to read the Bible in English and take a more direct part in Christian worship. These 'Lollards', were mostly found in Bristol and the developing wool cloth producing districts. No record of any violence or dissent exists for Shaftesbury, but a Shaftesbury merchant, Richard Ffowell or Voughell, was involved in the dispute that resulted in the burning of Sherborne Abbey and the Abbess and nuns must have been dismayed to hear of the murder in 1450 of their Bishop and the attack on Salisbury Cathedral.

Discontent with religion continued into the next century, but the Abbey was apparently unchanged. Its last crowned guest was Henry VII in 1491 and the last royal visitor to stay at the Abbey, Katharine of Aragon (the bride-to-be of Prince Arthur, Henry VIII's older brother), was entertained with great pomp as she made her first journey through England in 1501. Later the Abbey contributed enormous sums to finance the Field of the Cloth of Gold, Henry's excursion into war with France.

As Shaftesbury is often described as an ancient town it is surprising that there are so few Medieval buildings compared with, say, Salisbury. Only 'Edwardstowe' in Bimport is described by the Royal Commission for Historic Monuments as dating from before the Dissolution. A deed of 1496 may indicate the reason for this. A property

'Edwardstowe' has been in continuous occupation since 1500 or earlier. It retains most of its original roof and beams, two inglenook fireplaces, a staircase partially set into the thick stone wall and some 'plank and muntin' partitions (vertical planks slotted into grooved vertical posts or 'muntins'). These surviving stone doorways indicate that it was a building of quality, perhaps belonging to the Abbey.

Shooters Lane early this century, but looking much as it would have done in medieval times.

is described as 'a quantity of land, with stone walls' and, as these were unlikely to have been field boundary walls because they were in the centre of the town, they may have been the roofless remains of buildings considered suitable for reconstruction.

Among the interesting finds of the indefatigable Charles Mayo were these extracts from the rolls of the Courts Leet. From the 1471 Michaelmas Roll: 'John Gore, for allowing his hedges to overhang the King's way, called Pereswellane, and his mud to lie in the same lane'. 'The Rector of St. Martin's for timber lying next the Cross of S. John in Est (Salisbury) Street.' 'The Steward of the Fraternity of S. Gregory for stones and rubble from their tenements in Berton St. (Barton Hill). Thomas Palmer and Anabella his wife for entering the garden of John Wylkyns, on divers occasions, and removing thence wood and underwood . . . and the said Anabella as being a common scold and perturber of the peace of our Lord the King to the nuisance of her neighbours . . . and Margaret, wife of Galfrid Leverok, on a similar unruly charge.'

How unfair that their small misdemeanours should be remembered for centuries, when other people's are forgotten. One case that the Victorian cleric ignored and the Georgian Hutchins recorded only in Latin was of a Shastonian fined for building the 'mod. con.' of his house over 'Shetewellane': he probably saw little wrong in doing this as the surface drains of his day ran down this lane. One can mull over the origins of its name, hear the modern deep drain rushing down to the treatment works, and ponder this breach of Medieval sanitation rules when walking down Shooters Lane today.

Market Town on the Great West Road
1539-1662

On the 23rd of March 1539 the 650 year existence of Shaftesbury Abbey came to an end, which must have had a considerable impact on the town that had stood alongside it for all that time, but was not the death blow that has sometimes been claimed.

The nuns and people working directly for them must have been severely shocked by the closure of the monastery. Such servants' positions were often inherited and, as with people working for long established firms today, they probably had not believed it could happen. In 1536 when Cannington nunnery in Somerset had been closed and two of its eight nuns had chosen to continue their vows at

A view of the site of just part of the Abbey church shows the size of the building that disappeared completely soon after the Dissolution. The foundations were buried under more than two metres of rubble when the focus of the town shifted eastwards to where St. Peter's tower can just be seen.

31

This sketch decorates the survey of his newly acquired property made for the Earl of Pembroke in 1574. It shows the ruined Abbey with Holy Trinity beyond it in use as a parish church. It is the only representation that survives of Shaftesbury's great Abbey, except for what may be only a stylized representation on the Abbey seal.

Shaftesbury, it had probably seemed quite reasonable to everyone to abolish what in today's terms would be described as an uneconomic unit.

The impending closure had raised an interesting problem at Shaftesbury. One of the novices, who had been offered the chance to leave the convent because she was less than 24 years of age, was the daughter of the once powerful Cardinal Wolsey. John Clusey, the man who had been named as her father to protect the Cardinal's reputation, became anxious and wrote to Thomas Cromwell asking him to tell the Abbess to make sure that Dorothy Clusey did take the veil. It is not recorded whether she stayed voluntarily or was forced to take her vows, but she was among the nuns given pensions and still drawing it in 1553.

When a further wave of closures began in 1538 the Abbess apparently thought that Henry VIII, like previous kings, could be bought off and begged Thomas Cromwell that she and her nuns 'may remain here, by some other name and apparel, his Highness poor and true Bedeswomen, for which they would gladly give unto his said Majesty five hundred marks, and unto your Lordship for your pains one hundred pounds'. In a way she got her request for having surrendered the Abbey when the mixture of stick and carrot applied by Henry's agents became irresistible, Abbess Elizabeth Zouche and 55 nuns received pensions which enabled some of them to live together in Shaftesbury. It is not recorded at which church they worshipped or where they were buried, but as two of them Margaret Mayowe and Edythe Mawdlin, lived in Church Lane

Holy Trinity seems the most likely and it must have been painful for them to see their Abbey church being destroyed nearby. The Abbess and 44 nuns were still drawing their pensions in Catholic Queen Mary's reign more than a decade later.

For people less directly employed by the Abbey or leasing land from it such as farmers, shepherds, foresters or men who managed the estates, the change-over may not have been so noticeable. The land had to be kept under cultivation, sheep pastured and produce sold, or the value of the King's new possessions would plummet.

This need for continuity also preserved the market. Although town life continued, it must have been an uneasy time, with people wondering where Henry would turn next and rumours that he was about to take everyone's money as he had the Abbey's being readily believed. There must also have been considerable unease about religion, with the changes that many people had wanted for more than a century being suddenly imposed by a King who had earlier in his reign professed himself a staunch Catholic. The church guilds must have wondered what to do about their chantrys, as is revealed in a deed described by Hutchins. John Mathews, a member of a family prominent in Shaftesbury for many generations, wished to arrange masses for four years to be said for his late wife Ellen, but added the rider 'if the King's laws suffer'; if not the cost of the masses was to revert to Richard Mathews, presumably his son.

The other thing that probably disturbed at least the older people in the town was the rapid destruction of the Abbey that had so long been its great landmark. The destruction was deliberate, to prevent the re-foundation of the nunnery. Shaftesbury already had more churches than it needed, unlike Sherborne where the townspeople were glad to buy the beautiful church of the monks and pull down their own. In populous towns such as Bristol and Gloucester the monastic churches were turned into cathedrals for the new dioceses created by Henry. Shaftesbury was given the ex-Abbot of Milton as

The upper drawing is of a fireplace removed from the 'Crown' by its owner, the Marquis of Westminster and, as it was thought to have been a tomb canopy from the Abbey, illustrated in the Victorian edition of Hutchins. The lower photograph of the present fireplace, although described by the Royal Commission for Historic Monuments as 16th century, is different and appears to be a replacement put in when the 'Crown' was rebuilt in 1862.

33

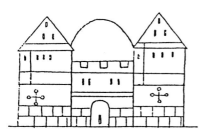

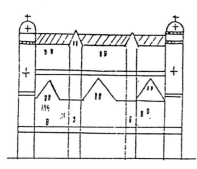

Three sketches used by the Rev. J. J. Reynolds in his 1867 book. The top sketch is of the house of William Grove (dated 1615), the two lower sketches are of the house of Lord Arundell (dated 1615 and 1620). The 1620 sketch may have come from a plan of the town said to have been made in that year and now lost.

a suffragan bishop, but nothing could save the Abbey church.

The descendants of people who had been connected with the abbey removed some items: a grave slab and the body it marked were transferred to St. Peters church. There is a possibility that the nave ceiling in Marnhull church may have come from the Abbey: it has the Carent arms in one of its compartments and there was a 'Carent Chamber' in the Abbey when one of that family was abbey steward.

Hutchins mentions Thomas Wriothesley, Earl of Southampton, as the first buyer of the Abbey, also that it belonged to the Arundells, but admits himself defeated as to whether 'The manor and the whole site of the monastery ever belonged to that family long'. His confusion is understandable. The first Sir Thomas Arundell bought the Abbey site, property in the town that had belonged to the Abbey and the adjacent manor of Barton from Henry VIII. A survey of his property made for him in 1548 by Robert Grove survives.

Sir Thomas Arundell was one of the men employed by Henry in the Dissolution, but he appears to have approached his job differently from the other commissioners and channeled appeals from some of the monasteries to his master with apparent sympathy, including that from the Abbess of Shaftesbury. However, when these were turned down by Cromwell, he was no less interested in obtaining the spoils than his fellow royal servants, such as WIlliam Herbert who bought Wilton Abbey and in 1551 was created Earl of Pembroke. Arundell was also involved in demolition of monastic buildings, which casts doubt on the theory that he bought Shaftesbury Abbey with the intention of returning it to the Abbess and nuns should the religious climate change. He was executed before the accession of Catholic Queen Mary would have made such a thing possible. On Sir Thomas's execution the Earl of Pembroke bought his escheated Shaftesbury property from the Crown. Pembroke does not seem to have lived here and leased it to Sir Thomas's son Mathew and grandsons Thomas and William. The 1574 survey of the Pembroke lands indicates that Sir Mathew Arundell had built the house at the corner of Bimport and Tout Hill, which was not listed on the 1548 survey.

A reason why Shaftesbury is thought to have been a ghost town after its Abbey closed is that it was listed in 1541, with a large number of other towns, as being too poor to pay the extortionate taxes demanded by a King still short of money. Whatever the truth of this assertion, Shaftesbury became accepted as a place so poor that the cellars of fallen buildings made traps for the unwary pedestrian. Reluctance to pay taxes, common as it has always been, was almost a speciality in Shaftesbury: in 1592 the people here were described as being 'very obstynate' and unwilling to be taxed 'according to their abylytyes'.

Probably at least part of the town fitted this description, but there were also signs of continuing solvency. Before the Abbey gates closed it had several inns, but now the number grew and the best of hem could expect the type of visitor who had formerly stayed at the abbey. The system of 20 mile stages or relays of horses set up to carry the Kings' messages was well established, and Shaftesbury certainly would have qualified as a staging point for horses – being almost exactly 20 miles from Salisbury and from Sherborne on the long established Great West Road. The horn of the guides who accompanied the royal messengers would frequently have been heard as they entered and left the town, and some care would have been taken that the roads were kept clear for the royal couriers, as well as other riders.

The inns not only catered for travellers, but also for those attending the weekly markets and twice-yearly fairs. Accommodation at every level would have been needed by people who came quite long distances to buy and sell, down to the smallholder who walked in to sell perhaps just one beast or the week's butter and needed something to eat and drink before starting the long walk home. Thus Shaftesbury got its reputation as a place with more beer than water as inns and alehouses proliferated, even the small ones brewing their own beer.

The 'Angel' on the corner where the post office now stands, and the nearby 'Antelope' welcomed travellers from Salisbury and the east. The 'Ram' and the 'George' were the first that travellers who had surmounted Tout Hill would see. Around the market the 'New Inn' had appeared on the Commons by 1553, with the 'Star', which belonged to Eton College, beside it. Opposite the older 'Swan', therefore on the south side of the High Street approximately where Nos. 29-31 are today, was the 'Bush'. While on the top of Gold Hill, where William Ketylton's house had been, the 'Lamb Inn' had now been built. These are some of the inns known from documents, there were probably many small taverns whose names have not survived, all of which would have served a thriving market by not only providing refreshment, but also a place where people could meet, discuss deals and make bargains, out of the draughts that blow on this 700 foot hill.

Shaftesbury's markets and fairs, like the surrounding country and its produce, were very varied. The part of the High Street by St. Peters church was known as Cornmarket and in it stood Oatmell Row, indicating the selling place for the cereals grown on the chalk downlands in increasing quantities with the aid of manure from flocks of sheep. The sheep were penned for sale in Bleke Street and on Gold Hill, which was also the pig market. Cattle from as far away as Wales were grazed on the Park to recover from their long walk, then sold in Bimport. The Fish Cross, a stone building with a lead roof that was a fish market, stood on the site of the present Town Hall and was presumably supplied mainly from Poole, which regularly sent fish much further inland. Bones from large ling and cod, also oyster shells, found in an excavation under a house on Gold Hill are thought to date from between 1600-1700, also the

An 18th century sketch showing Edmund Bower's New Guild Hall and St. Peter's church. The hall was a building typical of Shaftesbury at that time: stone ground floor with an oversailing timber upper floor, probably plastered externally. The Corporation met upstairs, the open lower floor providing shelter for market people.

bones of a cooked peacock, so Gold Hill was a place where people lived in style as well as being a market street.

Edmund Bower, mayor of the town in the 1550's, provided the market with shade and shelter for selling other perishable goods, such as the butter and cheese brought up from the Blackmore Vale, by building another covered market in the centre of the Commons known as the Poultry or Butter Cross. Shaftesbury's market did not conform to the pattern found in many towns where a large square, laid out by the original proprietor, was later filled in by stalls that gradually became permanent. Here the market was on the Great West Road, described as 'a common way for carts, carriages and all travellers from London to the Mount westwards' and very narrow, especially when in 1569 Edmund Bower built the town a new Guild Hall in the roadway alongside St. Peters church.

The market facilities that Edmund Bower presented to the town were not entirely beneficial to the burgesses, because they seem to have drawn Queen Elizabeth's attention to the fact that they were collecting market tolls. An enquiry held in 1585 at Sturminster, one of Shaftesbury's rival markets, not surprisingly found these tolls

belonged to the Crown. The privilege (and profit) of collecting them was then farmed to John Budden or Boden and James Sharrock who acquired the right to lease out the buildings and common lands, while Londoners Theophilus Adams and Thomas Butler acquired the right to hire out the stalls and butchers' shambles.

Adams and Butler appointed William Gower, described as a yeoman of Shaftesbury, to look after their rights, an appointment the mayor and burgesses were to regret in more than forty years of expensive court cases instigated by Gower or his son Nicholas, who inherited his interests and also farmed the Shaftesbury property of the Lords of the Manor, the Earls of Pembroke. The town may have thought that it had won when in 1604 it obtained a Charter of Incorporation from James I confirming what Shastonians thought of as their immemorial rights, but three years later Nicholas Gower reported the mayor and burgesses to the Attorney General for taking 1d for every 'way' of 30 pounds of wool and tolls on other merchandise sold in the market, also taking rent for about 50 stalls and shambles which were set up on the 'King's soil'. The documents detailing this and numerous other cases give interesting information about the Elizabethan and Jacobean town. More than 25 profitable flesh shambles stretched from the 'Olde Guylde Hall' near Park Lane, northwards to 'le Clemale House', which was possibly on the site of No. 11 High Street, where a butchers shambles is mentioned as late as 1817.

A curious belief is revealed in one dispute regarding beef: the mayor had been taking a fore rib of beef as a penalty from any butcher at the St. Martin's fair who 'kill and put to sale anie bull's flesh without beateing the bull' as 'bull beefe, unbaited is declared to be unhollsome in the booke of assise for bakers, etc., published by the Lords of His Majesties Counsell'. This horrible custom could account for the tradition that there was a bull ring in the area where the present Town Hall stands.

In addition to watching the mayor and burgesses for every breach of regulations and trying to prevent ordinary townspeople, such as

In 1604 Shaftesbury was proud to receive its new Borough Charter and celebrated by having a new mace made with the shield of arms of James I. As the actual mace is similar to the earlier one it is possible that two iron and silver shafts and heads were made at this time and the older arms plate transferred.

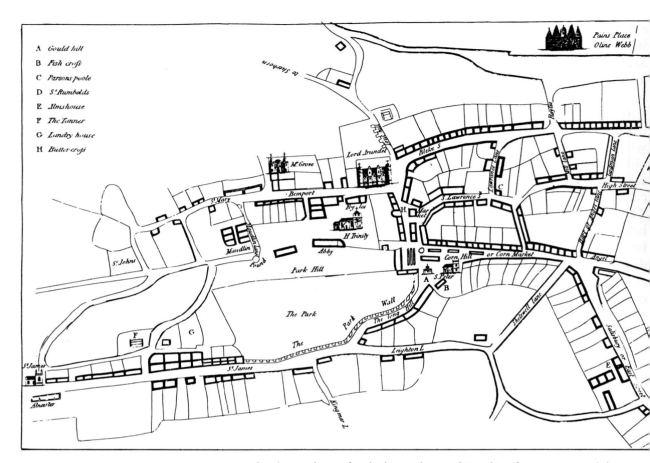

A   *Gould hill*
B   *Fish cross*
C   *Parsons poole*
D   *St Rumbolds*
E   *Almshouse*
F   *The Tanner*
G   *Landry house*
H   *Butter cross*

Part of a plan re-drawn for the later edition of Hutchins from an original that
subsequently disappeared. It shows a street plan very similar to the present one,
with many of the names recognisable. Barton Hill is marked 'High Street', but this
is possibly an error as both 'Berton Street' and 'High Street' appear on documents
of the 1400's. Only the Fish Cross and Butter Cross are labelled, although what
must be the New Guild Hall is shown parallel with St. Peter's. All four churches
are shown with towers at their east ends so, although each is drawn individually,
they may not be representational, as at least St. Peter's, and Holy Trinity had
towers to the west of their naves. The only inn named is the 'Angel', but what
looks like the New Inn or Red Lion is shown west of the Butter Cross. Some Abbey
buildings remain, one marked 'Abby', also the 'Maudlin'. The laundry house is
shown on the springline above St. James, which may have been the well and
laundry described in the Pembroke Survey.

Hugh Gibbes of the Lamb on Gold Hill, from taking a 'shew'
penny for any stall set up on the road outside their premises.
Nicholas Gower harried the traders in the weekly market that in
1620 stretched all the way from the Star to Mustons Lane. He took a
pound of candles for their standing from the chandlers and two iron
pins from a smith, 'to the great clamor of the cuntrye', and it was
reported by a trader called Longman that Gower (or more probably
his servants) took by force 'six knives and a paire of cardes because
hee refused to pay for his standing'. The 'paire of cardes' were for

38

carding wool for spinning and were like a flat brush with bristles of wire and a stiff leather back. Cards seem to have been a speciality of Shaftesbury tanners, who were known for the production of the stiff leathers suitable, not only for cards, but also for harness and shoe soles.

Another custom described in a court case was the payment of 2d per load for salt brought to the St. Martin's fair in November for the winter salting down of meat. The bailiff, 'time out of mind', probably therefore back into the times of the Abbey, had welcomed the salt traders with bread and beer, whereupon 'the owners of the salt carts have usually given the Bailiff a peck of salt out of every cart'. The salt probably still came all the way from Arne so the bread and beer would have been welcomed by the traders. When Gower interfered with such long standing customs a regular hornets' nest was disturbed. By 1620 the town was desperate to escape from his irritations and asked Lord Arundell to try to get the Dowager Countess of Pembroke to let the mayor and burgesses take the farm of the markets at a reasonable rent. This did not apparently succeed, and the disputes about the market only faded as the greater disputes of the Civil War commenced.

In 1626 the rector of St. Peters was in dispute with Henry Clarke, a Marnhull butcher who had a stall in the market. The Rector claimed a tithe on the stall, the butcher denied this right, brought forward a number of witnesses who had rented stalls over many years and all affirmed that tithes had never been paid. Clark's defence also referred to market stalls at Northampton and London not paying tithes and the Rector lost this attempt to increase his meagre living.

The market, including all the small traders and services that contributed to it, was Shaftesbury's biggest industry. Although some weaving was carried out, the town never became so involved in producing any one particular wool cloth that when the fashion changed half its population were out of work, as happened in many towns in the south west. There was still a mill for fulling broadcloth at Melbury Abbas owned by the Grove family in 1629 and there are references to 'Swanskin' and 'Linsey wolsey' being made here; the first a coarse wool baize used for soldiers' uniforms and the second a blue and white striped mixture of wool and linen used for bed ticks and working clothes.

'As well for themselves, but especially on the behalfe of the poor people inhabiting w'thin the saide Towne. The said Towne hath been continually vexed with suits in lawe for and concerning the Bouchers shambles, ffyshe Crosse and sheep pens by the space of 30 yeere at leaste by Gower the father and Gower the sonne (as informers) to the utter impoverishing of the said Towne.

'The Towne by reason of those vexations is growne aboue 200 li, in debte, there are above 300 begging people to bee releaved, and there are not above thirty howseholders in all the towne able to give

In addition to the poor rates to which everyone in the parish had to contribute, St. Peter's church had this oak poor box for contributions. It has three locks ensuring that the Rector and both churchwardens had to be there when it was opened.

releiffe.'

This letter that the mayor and burgesses sent to Lord Arundell, their powerful neighbour, emphasises, not to say exaggerates, the problems Shaftesbury and towns all over the country were having with the poor and unemployed. It is often claimed that these problems stemmed from the Dissolution, but it was more likely that people not needed on newly enclosed farms as agriculture became more efficient came to Shaftesbury in search of work or charity. Shaftesbury would have been a magnet to such people, as well as having its own resident poor and elderly in need of help.

These problems were tackled by the Elizabethan Poor Laws. Trying to halt change proved useless and training the unemployed in current skills was about as useful as it is today, as there was a shortage of work. Measures to prevent people moving about were also brought in, leading to centuries of misery as the old and sick as well as troublesome vagrants were chased back to the place where they were born. Shaftesbury took precautions against adding to its dependants after parish poor rates were introduced in 1572: Mayo found 33 bonds dating from 1587 to 1645 in the Town Chest labelled 'to have the Burrow harmless'. They were deposited by people who wanted to come and work or trade in Shaftesbury and had put up money as a surety that neither they nor their families would become a charge on the town.

In 1626 John Grove presented money for a workhouse for Shaftesbury and premises were bought in Parsons Pool. Its stated object was 'setting to work the strong and able poor, and for the correction of the idle and disorderly . . .'. Town accounts for 1629-30 indicate that it was used to train children (girls as well as boys) in useful skills, as cards and 'turns' (spinning wheels) were purchased. Payments to the children are recorded, perhaps for their keep, implying that they did not live in. Workhouses or 'Bridewells' were not effective, as their produce gave unfair competition to other workers and the Shaftesbury workhouse seems to have faded out by 1660. The second aim, which gave these workhouses their other title 'House of Correction', seems to have been ignored in Shaftesbury, possibly reformation of the idle and disorderly was left to the institutions at Sherborne and Dorchester.

Shastonians could be practical, but people were not always unkind, even when laws were harsh. In 1630 Ann Chubbe went to work for John Frampton a farmer at Gussage St. Michael, but after three or four days fell ill and asked her new employer to let her come home to St. James. He felt sorry for her and was 'contented to convey her to her whome' but 'finding her weaker and fearful she might perrish in ye journey' wrote to the 'tithingman' of St James parish to give leave for her to remain at the farm. Sadly, Ann must have died for her burial is recorded in St. James that year.

In addition to help from the parishes the poor were assisted from town funds which used income from property held by the Corpora-

tion to provide food and clothing, also to run poor houses where those who could not afford any rent lived. For the rest of the century these funds appear to have been adequate to support the poor of the town, or at any rate no new donations are recorded until after 1600. The donations best remembered are those that specified the building of almshouses, because they acted as a solid reminder that the money had been entrusted to the Corporation, whereas doles such as penny loaves or annual allocations of fuel could be conveniently forgotten and the funds channelled to other uses.

Mathew Chubb founded an almshouse for women in about 1611. He was not a Shastonian, which is perhaps just as well because he was known as a very tight businessman in Dorchester where he lived and traded. His wife Margaret was a Grove and added to her husband's bequest land that had come to her from her parents and her mother's father John Budden, who had farmed the town's land from Queen Elizabeth in the 1580's. The sixteen poor women in Chubbs almshouse attracted further bequests for another century, and after some vicissitudes, there is still accommodation for elderly ladies at 'Chubbs' today.

The other major benefactor to those unable to support themselves was born in Shaftesbury, tradition has it in a parish poor house on the site where his 'spital' or hospital for ten poor men was built. This is quite likely as there was at least one hospital in Salisbury Street which was probably used as a poor house after the Dissolution of the Chantrys. Sir Henry Spiller also made his fortune elsewhere and the property he donated to the support of his almsmen was bought specifically for the purpose in and around Shaftesbury. The town nearly

A drawing of the market cross that stood where the Town Hall is now. Local historian, Father E. Jeanneau, noticed that the stone post supporting a safety rail across the end of Park Lane (photograph above) bears a strong resemblance to it.

A vignette of the porch of Spiller's original almshouse drawn for John Rutter's book on Shaftesbury, but never published before.

41

did not get its mens almshouse because Sir Henry Spiller backed the wrong side in the Civil War and, after his death, his property was sequestered. But the mayor and burgesses had already set in motion the building of the almshouse in Salisbury Street and sent a deputation to Parliament that was successful in retaining the bequest for the town.

Education also concerned the town at this period. William, Earl of Pembroke, gave Shaftesbury a building called the Maudlin, which had been used as the Abbey almshouse. The town spent £40 on refurbishing it and presumably started the school there in the five years before he died in 1630. His heir, Philip, took the deed back saying it was not properly made out – and kept it. William Whitaker the Recorder then bought a building 'nearly opposite the gate leading into the churchyard of the Holy Trinity' which he presented to the town for the grammar or free school, earning for himself a nice epitaph on a Holy Trinity church window: 'Good men need not marble, wee dare trust to glass the memory of William Whitaker Esq who died the 3rd of October 1646'.

The master was not provided with much of a salary for teaching 'any poor boy that was brought to him', but he was given a large house, adequate fuel and free repairs to the building (useful as frequent window replacements seem to have been necessary). This meant that he could make a living by taking in fee paying gentlemens' sons. The school lasted for 120 years and ex-pupils who had learned Latin there claimed that it was good, but there is no record of any working class boy being educated.

A charity that provided education, but not in school, was the 'Weavers Money' or Williams Charity. William Williams was said to have been a weaver, but in view of the large amount of money he left in 1621 was more likely to have risen to be a clothier. He apparently thought that two years at sea would benefit fatherless boys or boys whose fathers' could not support them, before they were apprenticed to traders in their home towns of Shaftesbury, Blandford or Sturminster. His will also provided for men in his trade and many other needy groups in great detail, even the boys seagoing clothes were listed: 2 canvas doublets, 2 pr of breeches of yard broad russet cloth, 2 pr of stockings of the same, 2 jerkins of the same, 2 pr of shoes, 3 shirts, 3 coarse falling bands (collars), and 1 Monmouth cap (a moulded felt hat made in Monmouth).

Any nursing the Abbey had provided was lost at the Dissolution and people were nursed at home by servants or family. Only the poor with plague or smallpox were taken to the pest house and that was less for their good than to protect other people from infection. In 1629 the town expenses included 'reed to thatch the pest house', no doubt found to be leaking the previous year when William Whiteway of Dorchester recorded in his diary 'the 3rd of May the sickeness broke out in Shaftesbury,' but 'there died not above some 20 persons in all'.

The waterless state of Shaftesbury that visitors exclaimed about may simply have been the absence of the river or stream that was the reason for the existence of most towns. A number of wells have been found, five under the site of the Angel Inn for instance, which may have been in use at this period, but they are difficult to date. Parsons Pool was quite recently found to have springs under the roadway so, although Hutchins described it as 'a kind of reservoir for rain water used for washing houses', it had disappeared before his time and may have been spring fed.

In most towns, water carriers made a living selling water taken from a river, but Shaftesbury's took theirs from springs outside the borough at Enmore Green, which necessitated the payment of a curious annual tribute on the Sunday before Ascension Day to the Lord of the Manor of Gillingham. The tribute comprised the best local produce: ale, 'white wheaten bread', a calves head, also gloves, which were highly regarded gifts. There was also the mysterious 'Bezant' or 'Byzant', the name of which suggests a gold coin or a tribute, but was described as 'like a May garland with gold and peacocks feathers'. The Mayor was required to walk in procession down to the wells and present the five tributes, the Byzant itself being given back to him. The origin of the ceremony is said to be lost in the mists of time, but the first reference I have found is a bill of 1655: 'Item To the balie of Gillingham for our accostomed liberty to fetch water in Motcomb 1 payr of gloves at ye prse of 6s, and a calves head 8d, in beere 1s, and bread 2d.' Curiously, this was during the Commonwealth when most activities of this kind were suppressed.

The fact that Shaftesbury's water supply was so obviously limited may have contributed to its escape from serious fires by making people more careful. Widespread fires, often consuming a whole town or village, were frequent in the centuries when thatch was the commonest roofing material. The effects could be particularly serious for market towns: if the market ceased even for a few weeks and people acquired the habit of going elsewhere the economic base of the whole town could be ruined. Shaftesbury had crooks to pull off thatch to prevent the spread of fire and, as an even more effective precaution, it paid John Freke £1 a year during the Commonwealth period for 'looking to the Chymnyes about ye towne', presumably making sure that they were safely built and maintained. Also there was the curfew, rung from St. Peter's at 8 o'clock, to remind people to make their fires safe for the night.

In the reign of Charles I Shaftesbury suffered several epidemics, causing hardship and relief from taxes. The presence of goldsmiths suggests that they were not too serious. Some family businesses continued over several generations: the 1629 Midsummer Sessions in Shaftesbury approved the 'privileges belonging to an inn' to the 'ancient house' of Albinus Muston which he claimed had been 'an house of entertaynment of travailers men and horses, but principally

An implement in Shaftesbury Museum that may have been one of the town crooks used to pull down thatch in case of fire.

One of the 'chymnyes' that John Freke may have inspected still stands in St. James Street.

on the market days, by the space of three score years or upwards, and an hause of great receipt'. An Ethelred Muston recorded in Coleman Lane in the 1540's was probably his father or grandfather and Albinus had extended the family inn to take 'an hundred horse on any market day'.

The Mustons were not the only family whose prosperity in one occupation continued through the generations. Another family that gave its name to a lane were the Haimes, who had a horse mill in what is shown as Mille Lane on the 1615 map. Various Haimes were also millers at the watermills at Gillingham and French Mill between 1500-1700.

The Protestant religion that evolved after the Dissolution was a less flamboyant one in which services had their focus in a centrally placed holy table that everyone could see, rather than a screened off altar in the chancel. When a bishop with leanings towards church ritual ordered rails to be placed round the communion table and its removal to the east end of the church, making it in effect an altar, the churchwardens of Beckington were willing to go to prison rather than comply. At Shaftesbury, in the same diocese, there is no record of the reaction to this command and the 1631 communion table is still in use in St Peter's. Indeed there is little evidence of religious opinion, Mayo only found one derogatory reference in 1632 to William Hopkins being a 'Brownist' (a member of a particular puritan sect) therefore refusing to attend church – and he was the hated Nicholas Gower's son-in-law. St. Peters church was the ideal shape for this type of service, being almost square and having no separate

The earliest surviving house in St. James, probably built between 1600 and 1650, has the typical 17th century through-passage leading from the front door to the back, the bay windowed parlour on the left and the hall with its big inglenook fireplace in the centre of the house. Probably originally the home of a prosperous farmer.

chancel. The walls must have looked scarred when altars and screens were removed and there is evidence that panelling was used to dignify the church. This would have produced an impressive, if sombre effect with the oak pews that filled the church. Each member of the congregation now had their allotted place: the better seats paid for, the back ones for the poor. A typical seating plan of 1577 survives for Compton Abbas church.

There were no notable Civil War battles in the vicinity of Shaftesbury, nor did it have the misfortune to be burnt or sacked, but it constantly had troops of horsemen charging through. This may be why chains were purchased to stretch across 'Toott Hill, the Ames Hous (Chubb's, Salisbury Street), Bimport, Saint James' Hill and Copstreet Lane' and two more bought later, which were perhaps for Bleke Street, Bell Street or Gold Hill? Possibly people thought the chains might slow down cavalry, giving them time to clear the streets or get down their thatch crooks to deal with fire if their roofs were set alight. Any damage caused by the troops was in addition to the money the town was forced to pay for their upkeep. In 1627, when troop movements had been caused by war with France, a receipt was given to the 'Maior and Constables of Shasberrye' for £10 contributed by the town for 'one dayes conduct for three hundred soldiers of the Regiment of Collonell Conway'. However the main threat to Shaftesbury was to its means of support, the market. Possibly this is why the townspeople, unlike the Puritans in Dorchester, did not reveal their sympathies: a neutral town can sell

Ox House, Bimport, parts of which date from the 16th century. Until the 1950's it had a ceiling decorated with Tudor roses suggesting it may have been the house of Mr.Grove shown on the 1615 plan. It would have been one of the grander houses in the post-Dissolution town, the Groves being a prominent family in the service of Shaftesbury's leaders the Arundells of Wardour.

to both sides and, although in wartime normal trade is disrupted, extraordinary profits can be made. The only other reference to the Civil War was a payment in 1644 'to rayse a stock for powder and to paye poor men that go on the larums' and 'Paid for 4 quartes of whine for Capten Barnes', which may indicate that the wheels of business were even then being oiled.

The Clubmen were an interesting phenomenom of the Civil War: a 'pacifist' rising. Protest was not unknown in the area: people at Gillingham had risen against forest enclosure in the 1620's taking as their slogan 'Here we were born and here we stay'. The Clubmen originated in Somerset where 'farmerly men and others of the clergy' petitioned Prince Charles about the depredations of his troops. Later, when Parliament was gaining the ascendancy, a similar protest took place centred on Shaftesbury. They, too, had a slogan: 'If you offer to plunder or take our cattle, Be assured we will give you battle'.

Although life in Shaftesbury cannot have been pleasant, the citizens probably suffered less than country people and there is no evidence that leaders of the Clubmen came from the town. Probably the reason they dug themselves in on Castle Hill was that Sherborne Castle was under siege by the parliamentary army and it had a commanding position on the road by which reinforcements to the

Sadly these bells will never ring again, but they can be seen at close quarters at the Museum. The 1597 bell was bought for Holy Trinity at the end of the reign of Queen Elizabeth and the other in the reign of Charles I (1641).

46

besieging force would come from London. The more sensible of the Clubmen probably hoped simply to bring their protest to the attention of the Parliamentary leaders, the less well-intentioned boasted wildly about raising the seige of Sherborne and belied the stated aims of the majority.

The leaders were soon rounded up and taken to Sherborne, while Cromwell was sent to deal with a group that had assembled at Duncliffe Hill with the declared intention of freeing them. After speaking to them he went with only 50 men and tried to persuade 2,000 Clubmen (his estimate) assembled at Hambledon Hill to return to their homes. While the leaders were kept talking, some of Cromwell's troops crept round the back and the Clubmen were defeated. Cromwell concluded his report to Fairfax with the famous sentence: 'I believe (we) killed not 12 of them, but cut many and have taken about 300, many of which are poor silly creatures whom if you please to let me send home they promise to be very dutiful for time to come and will be hanged before they will come out again'.

Parliament also appears to have been wary of public opinion when the Arundell ladies and children were brought to Shaftesbury after Wardour Castle had been taken. They did not wish to keep them here where the family were popular, or take the inhumane step of sending them to Bath where plague and smallpox were raging, so they compromised and sent the two young boys to Dorchester and kept their mother and grandmother here.

During the Commonwealth Shaftesbury was described as 'a market towne of great resort and a great thoroughfare between London and the Mount and hath therefore allways had a constant weekly lecture'. Like St. Peter's rectors they found the stipend inadequate and ordered a supplement of £50 to attract a good 'lecturer' or preacher. One of the lecturers was Thomas Hallett who had been master of the Free School.

Pocket Borough
1662-1820

A note in the St. James register describes it as having been 'detained from the minister by Oliver Cromwell's Act from the yeere 1653-1662 so that by him there was nothing registered'. The tone of the entry suggests it was written by someone who welcomed Charles II's return from exile and wished to place the blame for any inefficiency in the parish administration squarely with the recent regime. Not everyone shared his Royalist sympathies. Thomas Hallett, 'lecturer' at St. Peters who now became its rector, found the re-imposition of a church hierarchy unacceptable and resigned with many other ministers on St. Bartholomew's Day in 1662. The next year he was convicted and fined with three others for preaching publicly at Shaftesbury to what was described as 'a riotous and unlawfull assembly'. However, supporters of the Presbyterian church that had been established under the Commonwealth continued to meet secretly, according to Hutchins, in a room in Crown Alley to listen to Mr. Hallett and other ejected ministers.

Crown Alley sounds as if it would have been off Mustons Lane and it was there, as soon as their meetings became legal in 1672, that Shaftesbury's first dissenting church was built. The Presbyterian manse in Park Lane, which was bought in 1700, is thought to be the oldest in the country. Although there were groups of Quakers in Dorchester, Bridport and Rhyme Intrinsica, they do not appear to have established a 'Meeting' in Shaftesbury until 1745.

Shaftesbury's four parish churches settled down to repairing the fabric of their churches, which had been neglected if not actually

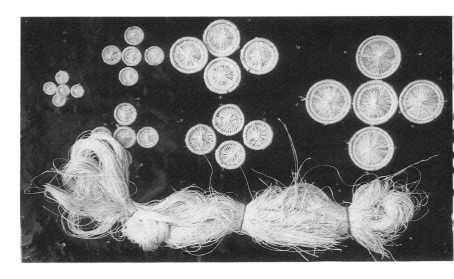

Dorset buttons contributed to the overall prosperity of Shaftesbury as women, children, the old and infirm could all keep themselves by making them. Early ones were made by covering thin rings of sheeps horn with fine linen stitched in a variety of ways with linen thread. Later wire rings were used as a base. A large cottage industry grew up and stitched buttons were made for two centuries before they were superceded by shirt buttons made on a machine first shown at the 1851 Exhibition.

damaged under the Commonwealth. The oldest bell in St. Peters (the second of six) carries the date 1670 and has the inscription: 'When I do ring prepare to pray', also what are probably the churchwardens initials RA and TB. The tenor bell (No. 6) was made two years later by Thomas Purdue and as the bell used to toll for the deaths of parishioners is embossed with the appropriate instruction: 'When you hear for me to toll then pray to God to save the soul'. The treble (No. 1), also made by Purdue, has the less serious 'A wonder great my eye I fix where was but three you may see six' referring to the former rule that parish churches were only allowed three bells; the three old bells were re-cast in the next century. During other repairs in 1674 a decorative rain water head was put up to take the water from the south aisle roof; it is preserved in the museum next to the church. At Holy Trinity they bought a silver cup and had it inscribed 'This chalic belongeth to the holy trinity of Shaston, 1670'.

The decorative rain-water head dated 1674 from St. Peter's.

The eighteenth century churchwardens' accounts of St. Peter's not only cover repairs and new purchases for the church, but bell ringing for all kinds of celebrations from fairs to military victories, also relief of poor travellers such as sick soldiers or sailors travelling across country to get home or to another port. The rector also received 'briefs' from other churches appealing for funds for anything from re-building a church to helping towns devastated by fire or flood; from these accounts it appears that Shastonians were generous to disaster victims, but hadn't anything to spare for other peoples' churches. All this money had to be collected by the churchwardens from the parishioners: a complete social service by two unpaid workers.

The attempt by the Duke of Monmouth in 1685 to gain the throne from Catholic James II, although supported by Protestants in the area, does not seem to have affected Shaftesbury as much as other places, but a small document that illustrates the effect such major disturbances have on the lives of people who take no part in them

A market town had to have accurate weights and measures. This bushel measure for cereals, possibly another product of the itinerate bell founder, has raised lettering: 'The Burrowgh of Shaston Lewis Evans Mayor 1670'. Another one was bought exactly a century later, but was much more portable, being wood with metal bands.

survives. It is a pass addressed to 'His Majestys Officers both military & civil' issued to a pedlar called Andrew Little certifying that he had been resident in Shaston for 5 weeks, 'hath not been in arms in the late rebellion' and wished to return to Scotland. (Incidentally, he was given 42 days to complete this journey).

A legacy from the Commonwealth that soon benefited Shaftesbury was the post office organization initiated by Cromwell. Shaftesbury had its first post master by 1667, a Captain Fry who, curiously, lived at the 'Angel Inn' which stood on the site of the present post office. Dorchester, although the county town, did not have a post office for another 30 years.

Stage coaches were already in operation, but they were little faster than the stage wagons that plodded from place to place carrying goods as well as people, so the mail was carried by post boys on horses for another century. The road that riders, pack ponies, covered carts and coaches took from Salisbury can still be walked high on the downs. Daniel Defoe writing about 1720, but at the end of his life and drawing on memories of journeys when he was a younger man, describes this route from Salisbury to Shaftesbury as it had been for centuries: 'over that fine down or carpet ground, which they call particularly, or properly Salisbury Plain. It has neither house or town in view all the way, and the road which often lyes very broad, and branches off insensibly, might easily cause a traveller to loose his way, but there is a certain never failing assistance upon all these downs for telling a stranger his way, and that is the number of shepherds feeding, or keeping the vast flocks of sheep, which are everywhere in the way, and who, with a very little pains, a traveller may always speak with. . .'

Most of the inns from the previous century were still going, except Albinus Muston's 'Crown', which may have changed its name to the 'Running Horse' during the period when crowns were out of fashion. The 'New Inn' had become the 'Red Lion' and was the leading inn. It was evidently large as, not only did the mayor and corporation drink the health of Queen Anne there in 'clarett and sacke' when she came to the throne in 1702, but the ordinary townsfolk also gathered there to celebrate her accession. At her coronation, however, the Corporation adjourned to the 'Katherine Wheele' for their drinking, perhaps because Peter Pike its innkeeper had offered his field, Castle Hill, as the site for the bonfire. Innkeepers commonly rented fields near the town to graze the horses they hired out. The Corporation spread its patronage among the inns. The Bishop on his annual visitation was dined at the 'Mitre' (still on the same site today) in 1725 and the 'Five Bells' a little further down the same side of the High Street in 1726.

However, what might be termed saturation point had been reached with over 27 inns or alehouses in a town of no more than 1,000 people. The decline of several inns can be traced through their being listed as empty in St. Peter's parish accounts. The 'Lamb', which belonged to the town, was empty in 1725 and became one of the properties used officially to house the poor. The 'George' also became housing for the poor: its large yard and many outbuildings split up to make cheap lodgings and workshops for numerous lowly work-people, women as well as men, at considerable profit to its owner. Lord Arundell's great house seems to have ended its days as part pub (the 'Rose & Crown') and part workshops.

'The Star', next door to the 'Red Lion', belonged to Eton College and had a long existence. In 1743, when innkeeper Stephen Stickland died, a complete list of the contents was made. As well as pewter plates and mugs for serving food and drink, the kitchen was equipped with various brass utensils. All the equipment for brewing was listed in the brewhouse and cellar. Eleven beds are recorded altogether, but remember that inn beds frequently held more than one or two people. They were listed in various rooms including the 'Kings Arms Chamber', even one in the dining room. Not only were most of the beds complete with fine goose feather beds and bolsters, but there were the refinements of a 'tea kittle' in the kitchen and seven prints and two maps on the walls of the dining room, so this was quite a sophisticated inn.

Other lists of house contents made at this time reveal that compared to those of the 'Star' the items in the home of widow Hamanalin Sealy of Shaston who died in 1736 were more limited, but like most old ladies she had accummulated a lot of linen. Her wearing apparel was the most expensive item by far at £2, which with books (5/-) and a 'tea ketel' suggest gentility. She also had a 'chestadrors'!

Changes were taking place: Oatemell Row was taken down in 1684 and its lead and other materials stored for re-use. Possibly it was the first victim of wheeled traffic in the town, as more space was needed to allow coaches and waggons through than had been required for the movement of men and pack animals. In 1727 the Butter Cross was removed from the Commons and does not seem to have been replaced, although Shaftesbury was still renowned for its butter. Probably it was also a victim of the need for more road space as it had stood at the hub of the town between the, then still flourishing, 'George' and the 'Red Lion'.

New charities set up in the town in the eighteenth century do not suggest the desperate numbers of unemployed people that measures taken in earlier or later periods indicate. Simon Whetcombe left only £50, but it was to be used to make ten interest-free loans of £5 for five years to tradesmen wishing to set up their own businesses, which when repaid could be loaned out again.

Another new charity of the early 1700's was a school for twenty poor boys and girls set up by the will of mercer William Lush. In setting up a school to teach the basic skills of reading, writing and arithmetic it seems that Lush realized that the free school was not providing for really poor children. His charity was also practical in

A big jug decorated for the 'Star'. It is unlikely to have been made locally, but was probably ordered from the Potteries. It is amazing that such a large and fragile object should survive the rough and tumble of inn life.

This stone with Edmund Bower's coat-of-arms was taken the short distance from the Commons to a garden behind No.28 High Street when the 1550's Butter Cross was taken down in 1727 and remained there until the 1960's when it was given to the Museum.

The actual pool is marked on this site at the east corner of Parsons Pool and Bell Street on the 1615 plan. Later in the century a bakehouse here was left by Sir Henry Spiller to provide funds for his almshouse. Fricker's bakehouse, which caught fire in 1707, stood on the site and in 1796 Frickers were still running the bakery, probably in this building. The photograph was taken between 1865 when John Smith leased the bakehouse from the Spillers Trustees and 1885 when Sarah Ann and Elizabeth Smith bought the property and rebuilt the corner as it is now.

that it paid for the indenture of the child when educated to a local tradesman or to the then-flourishing Newfoundland fishery, also clothing while at school and when apprenticed, which would overcome the problems that the poor faced when trying to give their children a good start in life. Only boys seem to have been taken, but Lush's school continued for more than a century in a building where No.47 Bell Street is today.

One of the items in the Town Chest that Charles Mayo found in 'an exceedingly fragmentary and imperfect state' he fortunately quotes in some detail, as it describes the night time policing of the town from 1667 to 1709. It was apparently the Common Cryer or Bellman's duty to call up three or four men to patrol the streets from 9 p.m. to 5 a.m. throughout the winter months. The Bellman received 20s for six months night-work, the four men presumably got nothing, unfortunately it doesn't say how they were chosen. Mayo's comment was: 'The peaceful Burgesses of Shaftesbury, shivering all through the long winter nights, up and down the exposed streets of that upland town, one of which bore the expressive name of Bleek street, deserve our commiseration, and 20s seems an insignificant remuneration for the unhappy bellman, on whom this duty devolved for half a year'.

Mayo also gives information about Shaftesbury's fire prevention services from a Corporation Minute Book. As the town was never

seriously damaged by fire they were probably effective and as well organized as anywhere in the country at this time. In May 1707 there had been a fire at Fricker's bakehouse on the corner of Parsons Pool in the centre of the town and the Corporation made generous payments to the water carriers who had helped contain the fire, possibly by using their buckets to take water from the pool. Payments to the water carriers at another fire in 1713 of 2s per horse suggests that water was being brought up from Enmore Green on this occasion. As usual 'our last fire' prompted improvements, the Corporation bought Richard Freke's ladder which had apparently been borrowed, it also purchased two more which were to be kept for fires and no one was to 'presume to use them for any Comon occasions', at the same time the town crooks were to be 'put in sufficient repair'. The fire engine was kept under the new Guild Hall and a bell on the end of the building called up the water carriers and any other townspeople who cared to help.

Buying the fire engine was one expense, maintaining it was another, but St. Peter's churchwardens took the job seriously and paid someone to look after it. There were also payments to the water carriers when the engine was 'played'. I assumed this referred to testing it until I discovered that Crewkerne's fire engine was played to celebrate various occasions such as Guy Fawkes night. Even though these eighteenth century engines were pumps there was no

The first mention of a fire engine was in 1744 when St. Peter's parishioners agreed to spend 'up to £40' on a 'large street engine' and hoped the Sun Fire Office would contribute to the cost. It could have been this one in the Museum, or would have been very like it.

The house in the centre, with the oval window over the door, is No. 65 St. James, a fairly well-to-do house of around 1700. It has the earliest type of Sun fire mark under the eaves (the Office opened in 1710) and unlike most of its neighbours has always had a tiled roof so would have been a better 'risk'.

question yet of drawing water up from a river or using long lines of hose to fight a fire, the leather buckets carried on the engine were still an important part of the equipment.

Two attempts to sell piped water in the town do not appear to have succeeded. In 1702 William Benson, who went on to be Surveyor of the King's Works, raised water from the springs at Wincombe by a horse powered pump and piped it to a reservoir near the site of the present water works, but abandoned it as unprofitable. According to Hutchins, the system was re-used with the addition of pipes to take the water 'to all parts of the town', though I doubt if there were more than three or four outlets. However, as the reservoir was open and the water untreated the general opinion that 'in summer it was seldom or never fit for nice uses, as for coffee or tea' was an understatement and people went back to their bucketed supply from Enmore Green. John Hutchins refers to 10 or 12 wells having been dug in Shaftesbury 'recently', 'the last sunk in 1739 at the east end of Park Hill being 126 feet deep'. He also refers to dead wells: underground cisterns to collect rainwater from roofs, including one at the George Inn which held 250 hogsheads. Some of these dead wells remain: I have seen one in Park Lane and there was one behind Castle Hill House demolished recently. Many of the masons and quarrymen in the town at this period probably regarded well digging as one of their skills and a useful sideline.

In 1662 the Byzant ceremony was moved from the Sunday before Ascension Day to the Monday as being more suitable, which it probably was, particularly in the following century when it developed into an occasion of civic pomp. There were bills for 'lace for the serjeants hats' appearing in the accounts in 1708, also 2s paid for 'watching ye bezant', which adds conviction to Hutchins statement that the Byzant was adorned with plate and jewels lent by the local gentry to the value of as much as £1,500. Quite why they should risk their valuables in this way is not clear, but is puzzling in the way that our odd means of raising money for charity will be to future generations. By now a 'Lord & Lady' were appointed for the day, the last married couple in the borough had the right to this honour and received new clothes to wear. The main expenses of the day, however, were for eating and drinking by the mayor, capital burgesses and their friends, which rivalled Shaftesbury's other annual civic feast at the election of the new mayor every September. Expenditure on these entertainments combined with the system of management of the corporation led mayors into embezzlement.

Shaftesbury, like most boroughs, had a 'close' corporation in which the 12 members, called Capital Burgesses, elected a mayor from among themselves and chose new capital burgesses to make up their number from among their friends and relations when a vacancy occurred. There were no municipal elections and the corporation was unrepresentative of the townspeople as it contained no dissenters and no women. At parish level also control was restricted to men who were communicants of the Anglican church, which again applied to the Justices of the Peace.

In addition to being administered by this impregnable ruling clique Shaftesbury's finances were in the vulnerable state of being entirely in the hands of one man for two years at a time. The mayor decided on expenditure including maintenance to the almshouses, school and other buildings owned by the town, roads, casual charity to townspeople or travellers, civic celebration of royal events (which had great importance in a period when the throne had known years of insecurity) and the two annual entertainments. The mayor became 'Common Warden' for the year after his mayoralty and administered the common property of the town, with funds that came largely from property bequeathed to provide support for the poor, to pay the bills of the previous year which he as mayor had incurred, with obvious opportunities for dishonesty.

The difference between expenditure on the poor and that on food and drink for the town's wealthier men always look shocking in the churchwardens and borough accounts. For instance when a sick man is given 6d and the bellringers twice as much for one session, or when the almswomen have less than £3 a year to live on and the mayoral feast, for 'the gormandizing and guzzling members of the body corporate', as they were later described aptly by Charles Bowles, costs £27.11.0. The disparity increased in the years from

The gilded wood 'Byzant' was saved by Lady Theodora Grosvenor after the ceremony was discontinued and given to Shaftesbury. It is probably the one for which Charles Pinhorne paid £17.11.0 in 1771, the year the feast cost £54.11.0 and all that was spent on the almshouses was 1/4d for whitewash!

Portraits of Sir Thomas Rumbold, Sir Francis Sykes, and 'Miss K—ghl–y' that appeared in the *European Magazine*. The picture of 'Miss K—ghl–y', said to be the daughter of a Shaftesbury innkeeper, was included because the magazine was stirring up scandal linking her to Sir Francis Sykes. Georgian political life seems very like todays.

1770-1785 when Charles Pinhorne dominated the Corporation and was four times mayor.

Pinhorne was an upholsterer who had grasped the opportunity offered by the increasing coach trade through Shaftesbury when the first turnpike road in Dorset was made in 1753 along the Great West Road, by 'fitting up' the old George Inn. In 1764 he advertised that the 'Bizant Festival' was to be held there. In his Common Wardens accounts Pinhorne shows no payment by him as tenant of Puckmore, the most valuable estate belonging to Spiller's Trust, no tithes paid to the Rector, no market rents to the Lord of the Manor, Lord Shaftesbury, no money spent on the roads and very little on the town's buildings. Foyle's charity ceased to be paid out and the capital disappeared, while places in the two almshouses were left unfilled. The opening of the Corporation Minute for 1785 has an ominous ring to anyone familiar with modern fraud exposures: 'Charles Pinhorne being absent . . .' and goes on to divert all payments away from the then Common Warden and into the hands of the current mayor and town clerk. But he seems never to have been disgraced, probably because such dishonesty was not unusual.

Not all the men in the corporation were dishonest however. Thomas Tucker, who was probably responsible for preventing Charles Pinhorne from continuing to enjoy the unjust fruits of his stewardship, was mayor in 1777, therefore Common Warden in 1778-9, when he received the bequest of John Bennett for the almswomen in Chubb's. Observing the fate of Foyle's £100 at the hands of Charles Pinhorne he kept control of this charity money and eventually passed on the hereditary trust to his grandson Thomas Boys Tucker in the next century.

Most tradesmen in the town, especially innkeepers, would have had no cause for complaint about the corporation's way of spending money. The diversity and general prosperity of farming in the area provided employment for professional men such as lawyers, land agents, doctors and surgeons. Together with the clergy and such of the townsmen who had prospered sufficiently in their trades to employ staff to do the more menial work, these were the men who became capital burgesses and ran the town.

Corruption in the 'close' corporation went hand in hand with corruption in the election of Shaftesbury's two MP's. Defoe, early in the eighteenth century, had dismissed Shaftesbury as 'now a sorry town', partly because it was not one of the expanding woollen towns he admired, but also because it was a 'Pocket Borough', where the MP could be bought. The small number of voters enabled the Earls of Shaftesbury and Ilchester to each have a nominee elected to Parliament by paying every voter between 5 and 10 guineas. In the 1775 election Sir Francis Sykes and Sir Thomas Rumbold, 'nabobs' who had made fortunes in India and were buying political influence and power by the aquisition of land and parliamentary seats, stood for Shaftesbury.

Part of a large political cartoon lampooning the Shaftesbury election when the voters were said to have received parcels of guineas ('goldfinches') from a man dressed as 'punch' for voting for Sykes and Rumbold. The Indian 'Nabobs', like most men who have made money, were begrudged their success.

Hans Winthrop Mortimer stood against Sykes and Rumbold and, not surprisingly, lost. He contested the results, a Parliamentary Commission examined 26 charges of bribery and corruption and awarded Mortimer £11,000 damages and Sykes's seat. This marked the start of a new way of controlling the electoral system in Shaftesbury. Instead of the carrot of bribery being used the stick of fear was applied: the fear of eviction from a rented home or business premises by the owner of the property. In order to control Shaftesbury voters therefore, Mortimer spent the £11,000 on houses in the Borough and began to put together what came to be known as 'the Property of Shaftesbury'. Compliant tenants benefited by having low rents and the Corporation received large 'considerations' or fees when would-be MP's leased any of the 50-odd properties in the ownership of the Borough.

Mortimer eventually sold out to Paul Benfield, who had made money as a Government Loans Contractor in the war with France; Benfield added to it and was elected MP in 1790 and 1796. When his dealings caught up with him and he was sued by the Treasury and Navy Board in 1800 the 'Property of Shaftesbury', by then more than 300 of the 400 odd houses in the town, was sold to Sir Mark Wood who spent £30,000 acquired in the service of the East India Company on its purchase. By 1808 he had sold to Robert Dyneley who also bought up the property of Richard Messiter from Wincanton. Messiter had acquired some of it by marrying Mary Brickle, an heiress of Shaftesbury, and some by collecting old buildings which he sub-

A drawing of 1791 showing the top of Gold Hill when the west door of St. Peter's opened onto a cobbled square with the market cross and stocks in the centre. To the left of the church is the roof of the Guild Hall and the row of Tudor buildings that stood in the middle of the High Street until the 1820's.

divided to make more 'votes'. For instance he divided what is now Nos. 12 & 14 Parsons Pool into five houses and built two more on the garden. Messiter also acquired great unpopularity in Shaftesbury by going broke and fleeing abroad. However, his memorial to his wife and three boys must arouse our pity as it was inscribed: 'Richard Messiter, who had the misfortune to survive them, caused this tablet to be erected.'

Robert Dyneley on the other hand was a friend of the town, lived part of his time at Castle Hill House and gave Park Walk to the inhabitants. He was said to have been out with his surveyor planning to extend this public walk when he caught the cold from which he died.

Some of this information comes from the Victorian edition of Hutchins, but the editors tactfully cease describing the somewhat disgraceful sales of democratic rights at the point where writs were issued against Mr. Benfield and coyly conclude: 'The estates in 1868 belong to various proprietors, the principal one being the Marquis of Westminster'. In fact when Robert Dyneley died his brother, John, sold out to the Earl of Rosebery on the eve of the 1818 election, the 282 properties costing him £62,560. The Earl appears to have been a bit tactless with the voters and found the Borough was not so controllable as he expected and soon sold to Earl Grosvenor (who later succeeded to the title of Marquis of Westminster).

The history of Shaftesbury may have taken a very different course, and its appearance considerably altered, if the object of the fifteen townsmen who met at the Red Lion on 5th February 1791 had been achieved. For Walter Whitaker, Recorder of Shaftesbury, Edmund Ogden the banker, Charles Bowles the attorney and lesser lights of the community such as John Imber the edge-tool maker were meeting, chaired by young Mr. Pew the surgeon/apothecary, to set up the Shaftesbury Coal Association. They intended to bore for coal about a mile south of the town. At this time the concealed coalfield at Radstock had just been discovered and drilling for coal struck men as a good investment. Unfortunately for them, but perhaps fortunately for Shaftesbury, no coal was found and their investment was not even repaid – despite the prediction of the engineer who had reported that he was 'satisfied that I can make the stinking blue slat pay all the expenses we shall be at in seeking for cole if we should fail of finding cole'. Presumably the 'blue slat' was oil shale, which was sometimes used as a rather unsatisfactory fuel.

St. Peter's was then the principal church and by Georgian standards was well cared for. The present 3rd and 4th bells date from 1738 when they were re-cast by William Cockey of Frome, the 3rd being described as 'now crazed' and the 4th as 'lately broke'. This cost £35.6.0. plus incidental expenses like 'spent with Mr. Cockey in

The former 'parsonage house' of Cann church, which was described as 'neatly rebuilt by the Rector in 1736' and has recently had its handsome central front door restored to use.

treating about casting ye bells 3/6d' and 'J. Hilbern for carrying ye clappers to Froom 1/-'. Another heavy expense in 1742 was 'hooping the tower' which cost £35.6.11d. As with bell casting it was unusual in that outside help was needed: William Monk of Berwick St. John was called in to fix supports designed by Mr. Price from Salisbury, but first the churchwardens travelled over to Berwick to 'see how their tower was hooped'. While he was here William Monk mended the all-important church clock – both clock, and bells were the cause of frequently recurring expenditure.

Another recurring and intriguing entry in the churchwardens accounts is for repairs to the 'Whirlygog', which I imagine to be some sort of turnstile gate. Several appear in a print of Wells Cathedral close and I think ours was intended to keep animals out of Holy Trinity churchyard: it frequently needed repair, children probably liked to play on it, so a padlock was made for it by Mrs. Harvey in 1737. It was replaced by an ordinary gate made by Joseph Hiscock in 1755. Another hardy annual in the church accounts was cutting the trees in Holy Trinity churchyard, probably the very lime trees that are there today – as pollarded trees live to an unusual age. This usually cost 10/- in money and 2/6d in beer, a considerable amount when labourers only earned a shilling a day.

The last of St. Peters bells was re-cast in 1776 by R. Wells of Aldbourne. It was inscribed, 'While thus we join in cheerful sound may love and loyalty abound' and the name of only one of the two churchwardens 'Hugh Oram'. However it looks as if love and loyalty did not abound in St. Peter's vestry: not only was there this curious omission of the second churchwarden John Mathew's name, but the church accounts from this period contain numerous alterations, remarks like 'not sworn' and in 1780, among a frenzy of blots and scratched out names 'Hugh Oram refused to let ye parishioners sign their names for their choice of Ed. Buckland as Churchwarden unless they would sign for himself to continue'. Among the parishioners whose names have been crossed through are John Mathew and ... Charles Pinhorne! Later John Mathew is called to account by the Vestry for an overcharge for looking after the fire engines so it seems likely that the dishonesty prevailing in the New Guild Hall next door was not unknown in St. Peter's.

Orams appear frequently in the records of St. Peter's, including Elizabeth Oram who took over the job of 'taking care of the clock and the chimes' for £2 a year on the death of her husband. Hugh Oram's name first appears as churchwarden in 1751 when 5/- was 'spent on parishioners when chose into the office'. It may well be that Hugh Oram was not just a cantankerous old man in 1780, but really had the welfare of his parish at heart, and the doubts he seem to have had about the young Edward Buckland may have been justified as Buckland, elected a capital burgess in 1787, went on to dominate the government of the town far more successfully that Charles Pinhorne ever did: not only by getting his friends and relations into the Corporation, but by filling posts like Receiver of Rents and Town Clerk with sons.

Like the Orams, the Upjohns appear in all walks of Shaftesbury life in the eighteenth century. The first Upjohn here was a miller at Cann in 1661. Another occupation requiring this type of ingenuity was that of stone mason and some Upjohns were masons, among them Edward, born in St. James in 1685, who graduated to clock and watchmaking. Describing his work in Shaftesbury, his son James wrote: 'He cast his own Clockwork, forged his Ironwork for making the Clocks, cast his own Bells, and engraved his own Clock Dial-plates; he likewise made his own Varnish for varnishing them, and was so very capital in these matters that he did them for numbers of the Trade in the Country round where he resided. In the Watch-way, he made his own Movements and Motions, and finished the Watches complete; he likewise made watch cases and springs . . .' Edward Upjohn took his wife and young family of six to Philadelphia in 1723, came back and spent the rest of his life in Exeter.

Edward's brother Robert was also a stone mason and his son, another James, and a Quaker, went up the social scale a little by becoming a surveyor. His son, born in 1770, was the William Upjohn who drew the town plan, following his father's profession and dissenting religious views. William's brother James was evidently not a dissenter as he became Master of Lush's School and married a daughter of the Rector of St. James's with the resounding name of Elizabeth Plantagenet Dryden Mitchell. Their son Richard was a pupil at Lush's School and served an apprenticeship with Richard Downs, a cabinet maker in Bimport, but found fame in another profession in the next century.

A Quaker Meeting was established in St. James's in 1745 and their light and simple meeting house still survives as a private house. Later an adjacent plot was bought and accommodation built for visiting friends and their horses: necessary as a great deal of travel was undertaken with a religion which employed no preachers and even encouraged women to travel to other Meetings to talk to fellow Quakers about their lives and beliefs. This cottage also remains, and behind it in the garden are the simple name stones of the Quaker burial ground.

The Presbyterians who had built the chapel in Mustons Lane in 1670 found difficulty in keeping their church going in the next century and the remaining trustees and congregation re-founded it as an Independent or Congregational chapel in 1732. Their system of having each chapel entirely self-governing is described in Hutchins as being 'more agreeable . . . to the spirit of the age' and was probably more suited to independent Shaftesbury people.

Shaftesbury's Wesleyan Methodist Chapel was founded by a descendant of the family of millers long established in Haimes Lane. John Haimes father was a gardener, but John worked for his uncle, a button mould-maker for the then flourishing Dorset button industry.

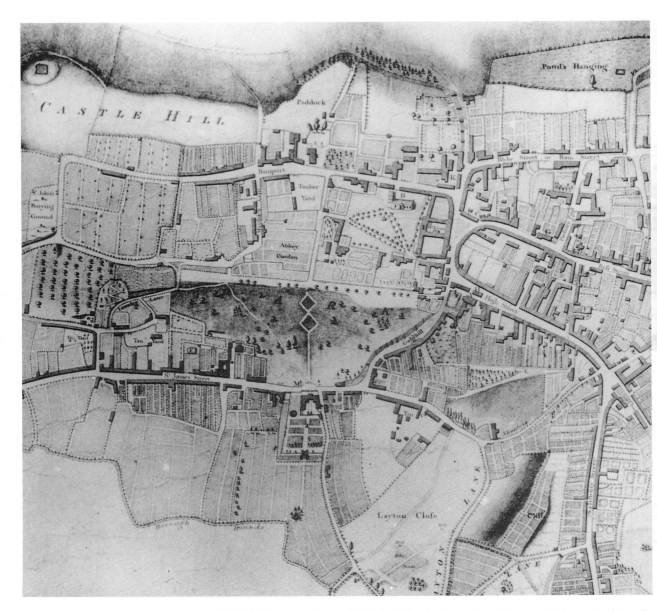

This is the central part of Upjohn's Shaftesbury plan of 1799, which was dedicated to the Lord of the Manor, Earl Shaftesbury. William Upjohn was born here in 1770 and knew the town intimately. He shows St. Peter's (A) as a plan, but Holy Trinity (B) is an accurate representation of the medieval church. He also shows the three non-conformist meeting houses: (E) the Quakers' in St. James Street, (F) the Presbyterians' in Mustons Lane and (G) the Methodists' in Bell Street. The old Guild Hall is marked (H), the Sessions Hall at the back of the 'Red Lion' (I). Only one house is named (K) 'late Sir T. Arundell's house', but he shows in detail the elegant Georgian pleasure grounds of the larger houses and the vegetable plots of the others. In 1988 the original copper plate was given to the Shaftesbury and District Local Hisotry Museum and larger copies of the whole plan are obtainable there.

A fine drawing by Samuel Marsh Oram published in 1785 by Thomas Adams, whose printing works was in the High Street. Samuel was a member of the Oram family who, having received an annuity, trained as an attorney and thus joined Shaftesbury's upper class. In addition to drawing he wrote some rather good poetry. The formal garden of the Elizabethan house on the south side of St. James Street can be seen opposite the double zig-zag path leading up to Park Walk, but the house is almost hidden by trees. The huddled town still looks medieval, but High House can be picked out and the houses on the south side of the High Street have formal gardens that run down the slope, some with gazebos from which to enjoy the view. To complete the elegant impression of Georgian Shaftesbury, in contrast to contemporary Wesley's 'cold uncomfortable Shaftesbury', are the ladies and gentlemen fashionably disposed in the foreground. Workaday Shaftesbury is idyllically represented by the men and women stooking corn in the field below Salisbury Street on the far right of the picture.

Unfavourable accounts of Haimes say he was accused of sheep stealing and joined the army to escape punishment, which seems possible as he left a wife and children in Shaftesbury, never to refer to them again in the autobiography written in his old age. He met Charles Wesley in London and joined other soldiers in starting a religious society in the army. Shattered by his battle experiences, he was helped by John Wesley after leaving the army and came back to his birthplace to preach in 1748. His preaching 'at a place at the end of the town where five ways meet ... upon a wall about 7 feet high', a place later adopted by John Wesley for outdoor services and usually assumed to be Angel Square, produced enough converts to start a society.

His preaching also caused a disturbance and he was imprisoned for the night, probably in the old lock up at the top of Gold Hill.

Later he was taken to a pub where he preached to the customers. Brought before John Bennett, the mayor, he was sarcastically told if he could work a miracle he would be released; the old soldiers reply, that he had already accomplished one by converting swearers and drunkards in the pub to God fearing men, gave him the last laugh, but upset Bennett and caused him to be imprisoned at Dorchester, from which he was rescued by two Shaftesbury Quakers. Further help in the shape of an offer of the services of two barristers and a solicitor to be paid for by a London man caused the local magistrates to drop the case against him, which gives a very graphic picture of justice in Georgian Shaftesbury.

By the time John Wesley paid the first of many visits to the town in 1750 on his way west it was said that the 'house contained four or five hundred people'. On his way back, after preaching successfully in the 'most riotous part of the town', one of the town constables came and told him that the mayor (Charles Pinhorne) forbade his preaching in the borough, to receive the famous reply that 'While King George gives me leave to preach, I shall not ask leave of the mayor of Shaftesbury'. And he did not, returning frequently and noting contradictory responses from the inhabitants over 35 years. Some of these, such as his reference to 'cold, uncomfortable Shaftesbury', probably refer to the weather, but with such a punishing schedule it is not surprising if he was sometimes discouraged: 'Preached to a numerous congregation, but wonderfully unconcerned. I scarce know a town in England where so much preaching has been to so very little purpose'. Nevertheless, he didn't give up and in 1785 was over 80 when he paid his last visit and, preaching at 9 a.m., saw among 'such a congregation as I had not seen there before ... the gentleman who, thirty years ago, sent his officer to discharge me from preaching in his borough'. He was a wonderful man, and I am glad his last impression of Shaftesbury was a happy one.

Other travellers also left contradictory reports of Shaftesbury, and the factor of whether our native greensand is dry or dark and dripping has a lot to do with this. A guide to Dorset published about 1716 says: 'the buildings are handsome being most of them of freestone', but later in the same book the buildings are described as 'but indifferent'. More than a century later Sir Stephen Glynne's February description of Shaftesbury is of a town of 'very singular and antique appearance' in a 'curious and romantic situation'. He is neutral about Gold Hill: 'very precipitous', but hates the houses 'of mean and irregular appearance' and invariably mentions the 'gloomy green stone' of every building he describes.

The 'Sun & Moon' Inn got its name from the Bowles family, who had long connections with Shaftesbury. Rowland Bowles fought against the Turks in 1593 with Sir Thomas Arundell of Wardour was knighted and given the sun and crescent moon, symbol of Islam as his coat-of-arms (the 'Sun & Moon' pub took its sign from the Bowles coat-of-arms). William and Anne Bowles enjoyed 70 years of married life in Holy Trinity parish to die in 1717, whilst Joseph Bowles was a Fellow of Oriel College and Head Librarian of the Bodleian at about this time. It is hard to see how such a job could drive him to drink, but unfortunately it did and he 'grew careless and negligent, lost his character, ruined his health, and died here in an obscure manner'.

The Rev. William Thomas Bowles chose Shaftesbury for his retirement and settled with his family at Barton Hill House in the 1770's, sending his sons to the Free School in Bimport. He is described as having 'planted and improved the spot' and the garden shown on William Upjohn's plan indeed looks pleasant. After his death his eldest son sold the house to William Bryant, one of the Borough Mongers, and wrote 'On Leaving a Place of Residence', a typically eighteenth century poem about the 'poor cottage' and its 'sylvan shade'. Nearly every sizeable house around Shaftesbury seems to have been called a cottage at this time.

His younger brother Charles became a well-liked attorney in Shaftesbury and was Recorder from 1804 to 1827. Charles Bowles was also a keen antiquary and probably the first person to excavate the Abbey site. In 1817 he wrote to the *Gentleman's Magazine*: 'Having obtained permission from John Dyneley Esq. the proprietor of the site of the late abbey of Shaftesbury, to make any searches I might think proper, I employed a workman to dig there, and at the depth of about 6 feet from the surface came to the floor, as I apprehend, of the conventual church.' He went on to describe the tiles and their heraldry, the fragments of monuments, 'not a single one with an inscription' and concluded 'Remains of the billety mouldings of massive pillars, of the slender Purbeck marble shafts, everywhere dispersed under ground, convince me that this once grand pile of building was composed of Saxon, Norman, and the modern architecture or Pointed'.

Like most of Britain, particularly the farming areas, Shaftesbury flourished during the boom years of the Napoleonic Wars. But the post war slump that followed brought unemployment. The curate of Holy Trinity, the Rev. G. Salmon, started a fund collecting money for a project that was beneficial to the town and provided work for which many local men were suited: taking down and rebuilding the retaining wall to the west of Tout Hill, also reducing the gradient on this difficult and narrow stretch of the Great West Road. Another new road, still the only new road in the centre of the town and called 'New Road', was cut through the north side of Bleke Street to make an easier descent to Gillingham and Mere.

Shaftesbury and the Grosvenors
1820-1918

The only surviving portrait of John Rutter, who died just before photography became common.

Two opposing figures feature largely in the history of Shaftesbury from 1820 to 1850: the man who transformed at least the appearance of the town, Richard, Earl Grosvenor, and the progressive and energetic Quaker, John Rutter. Both men were young and recently married when their paths first crossed. The difficulty in discovering what actually happened is that the Earl was represented by his agents and we know little of his real intentions, while John Rutter, with his stated belief that 'the great panacea is publicity', published his side of the story in great detail.

When George III died in 1820 Parliament was dissolved as usual and Shastonians got down to the excitement of yet another election. It was rumoured that Earl Grosvenor had bought their houses and votes from Lord Rosebery, but they were sceptical and assumed that this was a ruse to induce them to vote for the Earl's nominees. When they were convinced that the Earl was their new landlord they voted for his men, in spite of the introduction of a third candidate by John Rutter, as the Earl's agents made it quite clear that not to do so would put them at risk of eviction from their homes and business premises.

In 1824 the innkeeper at the 'Red Lion', James Shrimpton, was refused renewal of his lease, whether because he had been among the supporters of the third candidate or simply because Earl Grosvenor's agents wished to install another tenant is not known. James Shrimpton withdrew to the nearby 'Bell', which he had bought in 1822 and, as most of his customers followed him, the innkeeper of the refurbished and renamed 'Red Lion', henceforth the 'Grosvenor Arms', failed and left the town. Apparently even Earl Grosvenor was not powerful enough to decide where Shastonians drank, although he eventually bought the old 'Bell' and pulled it down in the 1850's.

However Earl Grosvenor was generous to the town as a whole and in 1826 gave it a new Town Hall to replace the sixteenth century Guild Hall that had been rather hurriedly disposed of for road widening. When he came down to lay the foundation stone he entertained the citizens in the status-conscious fashion of the time: mayor and corporation, gentlemen and leading men were to dine at the 'Grosvenor Arms', the rest were given free drinks at the 'Bush'. The arrangements were made by his agents and naturally some people were disappointed. Thomas James Bardouleau, a lawyer, made his indignation public by having his reply printed for distribution: 'I feel a most gross insult was intended . . . to billet me at the 'Bush'. I am neither a horse nor a tenant of Lord Grosvenor's. I have never eat

In this print of about 1850 by John Rutter's son Clarence the soon to be redundant water-cart can be seen outside the Town Hall. There is a gap after the 'Mitre' and another further along which were soon to be filled with new Grosvenor buildings. Two stage coaches are tearing through the town, but the fashionable ladies and the gentleman in the stovepipe hat gesticulating to the three yokels in smocks and gaiters, seem unconcerned.

The Town Hall, sometime between 1879, when the wooden clock tower in the photograph was erected, and 1923, when the existing stone tower was built to replace it.

(sic) nor drank at my Lord Grosvenor's expense, neither shall I do so now, unless at his Lordship's own table.' He finished up with some advice to William Swyer the agent, in Latin to show his superiority. Unfortunately he had it printed by John Rutter who, preoccupied with his own affairs, omitted to put his name as printer on the letter, a legal requirement.

John Rutter had received an invitation conveyed by the 'boots' of the 'Bell' with a list of the people with whom he was supposed to take wine at the Earl's expense. He must have realized this was a hoax perpetrated by the agents as the Earl would hardly patronize the 'Bell', so he wrote a pompous refusal and delivered it personally to the Earl's local residence, Motcombe House, obviously hoping to get the agent responsible into trouble. The Earl sent the letter to his agents to put the matter right and it was delivered to them at the 'Grosvenor Arms', where they laughed about it, giving Rutter cause for some righteous indignation later.

The foundation stone was laid, over a casket containing coins of the reign, on the south east corner of the Town Hall. While the townsmen waited for the Earl's arrival they gossiped about the events of the previous evening. William Swyer apparently thought he had got the worst of his encounter with John Rutter, so took revenge by acting as common informer and reporting the omission of the printer's name on Bardouleau's letter. Being mayor, therefore a local magistrate, he also decided to prosecute him for it.

John Rutter now found himself in the situation faced by petty criminals but, unlike the poachers and poor people whose transgressions were mainly caused by starvation and poverty, he had the money and education to fight back. He did this in the local court, in the County Court, and invited reporters to witness his court duels, even managing to get Shaftesbury affairs reported in London. No doubt local people who could not afford to challenge the close cor-

The 'Penny Whistle Band' was formed by High Street shoemaker Ben Strange in 1869. In 1898 George Hollis, a Salisbury Street watchmaker, became bandmaster and the band started to receive money to buy instruments and uniforms when the Prince of Wales visited the town in 1899. The band is still going strong and still wears the town colours of blue and yellow.

poration, the corrupt local vestries or the Earl's agents personally were delighted to watch the Quaker outwit trained legal minds such as Philip Chitty's, causing them to lose their tempers, if not their money, in court. In addition, for anyone too timid even to be seen in his vicinity, he published his account of what was happening in Shaftesbury in 'Shastonian Occurrences' and a magazine called 'The Shastonian' of which three issues were circulated and a fourth prepared before he was forced to cease publication.

John Rutter lost his cases and while the fines were not high the costs were, which may have been one reason why he decided to become a solicitor. Another reason was perhaps that he hoped he could help underdogs like his own office boy who, with two other boys, was accused of damaging the gate at the end of Church Lane (the successor to the Whirlygog?) and was told by the overbearing Philip Chitty at the trial that 'it is all one whether you did or did not (touch the gate); you were in company with one who did touch it, and that is enough'. The unacknowledged reason for this late change in career may just have been that when conducting his own defence he had found the cut and thrust of legal battles irresistible: he was in some ways not cut out to be a Quaker.

To take up the story of the Upjohn's again, the 1820's marked the departure of several of them for far countries. Richard, the cabinet maker and joiner, found it difficult to make a living and went to America in 1829, where he became not only an architect, but first president of the American Institute of Architects. His Gothic church at the end of Wall Street is still one of the famous views of New York.

The departure for America in 1830 of William Upjohn, the surveyor and his wife when they were both sixty years old, with five grown-up daughters and one old servant, is more surprising as they lived in some comfort at Cann Cottage. However it appears from his diary that as a Non-Conformist he was disgusted with life in England and his sons, William and Uriah, who had been in the States for two years, reported favourably on life and financial prospects there. Both sons became doctors and Uriah's son went on to make the family name a household word over there by inventing a successful pill making machine and founding the now enormous Upjohn Pharmaceutical Corporation in Kalamazoo.

These were the successful Upjohns. Others were leaving Shaftesbury under circumstances that reveal what conditions could be like for the poor in the town. Henry Upjohn was described as a gardener of 35 when he was sentenced to six months imprisonment for inciting William Taylor to break open a shop in 1821. In 1825, he was sentenced to hard labour for a month for refusing to maintain his wife and three children. With this criminal record he was transported for seven years for his third offence: 'suspicion of breaking open a barn and stealing wheat'. His son Elijah was only three

Charles Bowles in 1832.

when this happened so can hardly have picked up bad habits, but sentences had got worse when, at eleven years old, he was brought before Mayor Richard Buckland and J.B. Chitty in 1834 and given three months and two whippings for stealing a pair of trousers. At fifteen he was sentenced to six weeks hard labour for stealing rabbits and finally, at sixteen, went to join his father in Australia for stealing shoes. The only claim to fame the Australian Upjohns have is that Elijah, in prison again for larceny, volunteered for the job of hangman and became a participant in the most famous execution in Australian history: that of Ned Kelly in 1880.

John Rutter was not the only Shastonian to discover the iniquities of the close corporation. Charles Bowles, Lord Grosvenor's chief agent, had been Borough Recorder for nearly 25 years when he resigned as a protest in 1827. At the same time he dissolved his law partnership with Philip and George Chitty, men he had helped to rise from fairly lowly origins, as their grandfather had been Macebearer and their father Keeper of the Weighbridge. It is fairly certain that in 1831 Bowles wrote the anonymous book *Shaftesbury Corporation and Charities*, strongly criticising the management of the Borough in the past and the present. Another resignation in 1830 was of John Boys Tucker, one of the Capital Burgesses, but he hung on grimly to the funds that his grandfather had protected in the eighteenth century, until he could place the Bennett bequest in more accountable hands.

In spite of the apparent impossibility of defeating Earl Grosvenor's nominees in view of his hold over the majority of voters, some of the opponents of the close corporation clique, calling themselves 'Reformers' brought in Francis Charles Knowles to challenge Penrhyn and Dugdale, Lord Grosvenor's nominees in the 1830 election. Canvassing meant visiting every voter, election speeches were made in the street and, although only a few were eligible to vote, everyone from miles around came in to watch the fun, to boo and cheer. The meeting place was the Commons and the favoured station for speech making the balcony of the 'Grosvenor Arms', which gave a height advantage over anyone just using a carriage as a platform. When polling commenced, after nearly two weeks of campaigning, both sides made a grand entrance into the town: Knowles from Ferne where he had been staying with his friend George Grove, Penrhyn and Dugdale in carriages with the Earl's agents surrounded by servants in conspicuous livery and a bodyguard of gamekeepers and tenants from the Earl's estates at Motcombe and Gillingham.

At the hustings people complained of their treatment by the Earl's agents: a butcher called out that the Grosvenor agents had taken the bed from under his wife and children because he was late with his rent. Mr. Hiskins went on to say that he had offered Mr. Swyer £1 when he was at Philip Chitty's house 'in dishabille bottling wine' and that his fellow traders had offered to pay the other £2 for him. The

As the most prominent figure in the foreground of this 1830's print is a pig it is possible that this was a political print. One of Philip Chitty's speeches was interrupted by the squealing of a pig, which led to an exchange with Knowles about squealing and being tied by the leg.

Quakers refused to be intimidated. Beaven Rake, a linen draper, voted for Earl Grosvenor's men, but refused to take the affirmation to confirm his vote saying he would be acting in fear. When saddler Israel Mullett was asked to deny intimidation he said of Philip Chitty's canvassing visit 'Thy call upon me was purely on the grounds of friendship', but added that he had also been forced to sign a notice to quit agreement (later enforced).

The actual poll was taken in the Town Hall. The Mayor, who was also the Returning Officer, decided to deal with the disputed oaths behind closed doors upstairs and caused people to remark that it was 'getting like old Punch's elections'. Private details of Shaftesbury life came out when votes were disputed and both sides tried to prove disqualifications, such as receipt of parish relief by any member of the voter's family. This was embarrassing for one voter whose wife had received money from the overseers to pay for the confinement of an unmarried daughter. Any bribery was less blatant, but intimidation of the voters was barefaced.

Surprisingly Knowles got 121 of the 314 votes. Less surprisingly, in view of the hot August weather, and the feasting and drinking in full view through the large open windows of the 'Grosvenor Arms', which Rutter describes as looking like Balshazzar's Feast, was the window breaking that followed. The military were called in, but did not arrive from Blandford until the next day when all was quiet. There was still a reminder of this long-ago political battle in Shaftesbury until the 1970's. One of the evicted men found another property in Salisbury Street which he ran as a pub and carriers business, calling it the 'Knowles Arms' in defiance of the 'Grosvenor Arms' and its landlord.

Possibly because of Charles Bowles indignant resignation in 1827, the Corporation started to put its house in order. It made rather a show of curtailing expenses by such moves as getting Earl Grosvenor, the Lord of the Manor of Gillingham, to agree to the discon-

Another print by Clarence Rutter showing his printing office and chemist's shop opposite the Grosvenor Arms in its last years as a coaching inn. Over his door it says 'Stamp Office': when the penny post commenced in 1840 John Rutter's son immediately announced that he had in stock the penny black stamps. Like most chemists he made his own medicines. (see below).

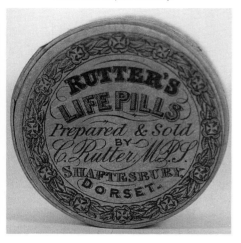

tinuance of the Byzant ceremony to save money. They also started some very necessary repairs to Spiller's Almshouses, later turned into a rebuilding for which the Corporation lent the trustees the money at 5% interest. After a Royal Commission investigation into Corporation expenditure visited Shaftesbury in 1834, Chubb's Almshouse was also rebuilt and the loan to Spiller's trustees made into a gift. This had the result that when the old close Corporation handed over to a more democratically elected body after the Municipal Reform Act of 1835 there was very little left in the kitty, in spite of a considerable amount of money having passed through the hands of the Corporation in the two previous decades. However, two impressive almshouses on the road into Shaftesbury from London proudly bore plaques recording the generosity of the old Corporation.

Although it was not until secret balloting became law in 1872 that all elections became really free, affairs in Shaftesbury improved with the 1832 Reform Act. The town lost one MP and the number of voters was increased to include people living outside the town. This made it less easy to influence the poll and by the end of the year a candidate put up by the Reformers was returned. The close Corporation having been made illegal the power of the clique was broken. For the first time all dissenters were eligible and John Rutter became a member of the Corporation.

Another major reform at this time was the removal from church

The rebuilt Spiller's almshouse of the 1830's in a photograph of about 1890. Behind the lad with the penny farthing that appears to be a little beyond his capacity is the 'Knowles Arms'. On the opposite side of the road was Chubb's, the womens almshouse, and a much plainer building.

vestries and town Corporations of responsibility for the poor and unemployed with the establishment of a countrywide system of workhouses. Anyone who was unable to maintain themself or their family had to go into one of these before they could be given any 'relief'. Unfortunately, herding the poor into large out of town workhouses, instead of the friendly, if insanitary, old premises like the Maudlin and the Lamb on Gold Hill, often led to hardship, especially as the emphasis on saving money and discouraging the able-bodied from accepting relief usually resulted in appalling conditions.

Col. A'Court, the Assistant Poor Law Commissioner who controlled the Shaftesbury Union, in a long printed statement to the ratepayers justifying his work, reveals a far stonger interest in saving money than making the lives of the poor bearable. A'Court solemnly stated that, when he explained to 'the labouring classes' that husbands and wives in the workhouse had to be separated because it was cheaper, they received his explanation with loud cheers, without realizing the irony of their response. John Rutter was on the first Board of Guardians and it is easy to see why he did not get on with Col. A'Court.

At first paupers from the parishes that were to be covered by the Shaftesbury Union were housed in old village poorhouses: the women in the converted cottages that had been the Motcombe

A rare photograph of Shaftesbury Union Workhouse or 'Alcester House' in which were incarcerated paupers not only from Shaftesbury, but also from as far away as Gillingham, Fontmell and the Stours.

poorhouse, the men at Gillingham. It took some time to find a suitable site for the new workhouse to be built and one negotiation had to be hurriedly abandoned when Earl Grosvenor realized the building might be visible from Motcombe House. 'Alcester House' was eventually built where Umbers Hill is now, in local stone some of which was quarried on site.

In the 19 volumes of the minutes of this institution there are some touching entries: from Mary Foot and her mother, who offered to maintain her brother's illegitimate child to save it from a workhouse upbringing, to an old lady's friends who 'refused to let her be taken into the workhouse'. For the sick poor the workhouse possibly provided better conditions than they would have had at home and subscriptions to the hospitals at Bath and Salisbury were paid so that paupers could be sent for special treatment.

The only 'outdoor relief' allowed was one off items like special food or blankets for someone seriously ill, or payments designed to reduce the number of unemployed by lending workmen money for tools, or such items as £1 worth of seed potatoes to start a man off in food production. There were payments for getting paupers right out of Shaftesbury: to Wales in search of work or, astonishingly, to Florida! One tragic family was even paid to come back from Manchester, where a son had died when they were about to emigrate to America.

Money could be made out of the very poor. Tradesmen competed to supply the workhouse and sold food to the poor in small quantities, on which their profit was greater than on the larger amounts supplied to the rich, who also got long credit. There was money to be made by letting out rooms in decrepit old buildings such as the 'George' Inn, or even purpose-building very small cottages. One house in St. James had nine cottages built in a small back garden between 1818 and 1845, which were known as 'Poor Yard'. 'Pump

In this view of St. James Street taken from the church tower in about 1900 the nine small cottages built on the garden of a house on the south side of the street can just be seen. 'Poor Yard' was sold in 1910 and the cottages gradually demolished, but two were inhabited until the 1950's.

Andrew's Yard (now Pump Court) was an insanitary court of cottages owned by James Andrews. Earl Grosvenor removed the front ones and replaced them with houses that show the influence of a national movement, strongly promoted by Prince Albert, to provide well ventilated and 'decent' houses for artisan families at rents they could afford.

Court', then known as 'Andrew's Yard', was also a warren of airless cottages named after the owner of some of them.

Another way in which the less scrupulous made money from the poor was by payment in kind. John Rutter describes Shaftesbury girls, particularly the button makers, being given cast off clothing instead of money for their work, which not only saved the employers money, but made it difficult for the girls to set up in business on their own account. He thought the comely Shaftesbury girls would look far better 'consistently clad in woollen hose, linsey coat and russet gown', but possibly at least the younger ones were happy wearing 'inconsistent, wasteful finery'.

The Ship Hotel, some forty or fifty years after Mr. Highman's day, with another group of men no doubt setting out for 'a day of the utmost hilarity', The hotel has a CTC sign indicating that it catered for those other pleasure-seekers of the 1890's: cyclists.

Men helped themselves when they were earning by paying into clubs which provided money to tide them over unemployment and illness, or even ensured them a dignified funeral. It is possible that the 'Hand in Hand' pub in St. James got its name from a friendly society as the property appears on earlier deeds as 'Club Houses', but more is known about the 'Hearts of Oak' which was a branch of a national society. The Oaks brethren had been pursuing their virtuous, if convivial, way for more than half a century and the four evergreen oaks planted in a member's garden yielded enough boughs for the brethren to carry at the funeral of John Chitty in 1821. John had 'in the hour of a neighbour's distress, nobly volunteered his life in a torrent of flames on the premises of Richard Downs (the cabinet maker), attempting to extricate a part of his property from the devouring element'. His fellow members hoped they would later 'meet as Oaks and enjoy with them the pleasures of eternal life.' On less mournful occasions they held business meetings at different pubs in the town and in 1849 'partook of an excellent dinner', at the Ship, 'served up in first rate style by Mr. Highman, the viands were good and the day was spent with the utmost hilarity'.

In the early 1830's a new and fatal disease spread from Asia into Europe. The disease was cholera, and as it was spread by contaminated drinking water it caused epidemics in towns whose water supply and sanitation were inadequate. Better houses and large institutions at this time had cesspools, often right under the building, from which water frequently seeped into nearby wells. In Shaftesbury, with its limited water supply, there were probably few cesspools, but outdoor privies or earth closets, kept relatively unobnoxious with ashes from the fires needed all year round for cooking, provided a far safer method. Shaftesbury's privies are shown on nineteenth century plans of the town, often built against the boundary as a semi-detached pair with the house next door. There are the foundations of such an earth closet in my garden: the door would have faced a fine view across the valley!

A small volume in the Dorset Record Office entitled *Shaftesbury & Cholera Morbus, Minutes of the Shaftesbury Board of Health* records its shadow passing over the town. Shaftesbury reacted to the threat of cholera in the same way as every other town by taking all the wrong precautions, which was only natural as the water-borne nature of the disease was not known. A meeting was called by the mayor and committees set up in each parish. The cause of contagious disease was then thought to be bad smells or 'miasmas' and these the committees proceeded with little difficulty to sniff out. We get a hint of the feelings that existed between parishes when St. James's rector reported no nuisances in his parish, but the drain from Gold Hill in St. Peter's 'causing considerable anoyance'. Before Christmas the poorhouses at the Maudlin and the old Lamb Inn had been whitewashed, a 'most offensive old drain' reported in Angel Lane, P.M. Chitty's houses are listed as needing attention and even the Earl's agents were to be approached regarding his property, in particular some houses in Layton Lane which appear to have been without a privy at all. Various pig styes were removed: one from outside Esther Harris's front door! Orders to Mr. Swyer to deal with

Gold Hill in about 1900. The old 'Lamb' inn, after over a century as a poor house, is boarded up and about to be demolished. But the area is anything but fashionable, hoards of children live in the tiny cottages and there are two doss houses.

The Shaftesbury Gas Company carnival float of 1912 posed outside the gasworks in Bimport. As electric lighting began to develop gas companies turned their attention to other things that gas could do. Cooking and heating were successful new departures, but the gas fan on the table came as a surprise to me.

A drawing of the gasholder from an early letterhead of the Shaftesbury Gas Company.

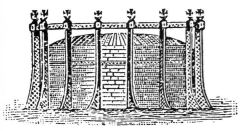

the cesspool in Thomson's Yard and to sink the privy in George Yard deeper and rebuild it seem to indicate that John Rutter's adversary was something of a slum landlord. Almost the last entry in this part of the book, before they ceased abruptly in January 1832, was to 'desire George Sheppard's family not to throw dirty water over the wall on Gold Hill'.

There appears to have been a further alarm the following August. The legally established Board of Health proceeded to use its new powers to take measures to try and keep infection out of Shaftesbury by putting up boards on the roads into the town warning off vagrants and employing beadles to hurry them out. Shaftesbury completely escaped the successive waves of cholera and in 1849, when Salisbury with its medieval drainage suffered the third highest death rate in England, the only record in Shaftesbury is of a thanksgiving day on which shops closed and collections were made for the poor at special church services.

The public service most associated with Victoria's reign is gas lighting, which arrived in Shaftesbury a year before she came to the throne. John Rutter had been complaining about the lighting of the town in 1826: 'just enough of oil and wick as would be most convenient to a footpad', and said it made Bell Street, quite a respectable address, a 'black slum' as it was beyond the rays of the lamp at the 'Bell'. He therefore joined other townsmen prepared to back William Morley Stears, a gas engineer from Stroud, who said he could light Shaftesbury more adequately and cheaply if the Corporation were prepared to let him dig up the roads to lay his mains. They were, he did, and a great deal of the correspondence over the ensuing century survives for someone to write a history of the little gas works, which was built quite proudly on the top of the hill for all to see in Bimport.

Religion in all of its many forms experienced a great revival from

78

St. James was rebuilt in 1868. This is the old church described by Stephen Glynne as having its nave not square with its chancel and side walls 'slanting very much'. The church was built right on the road, its replacement is further to the west.

the 1830's onwards, and churches were heavily restored or rebuilt. In Shaftesbury this followed the transfer of the whole of Dorset from the Diocese of Bristol back to Salisbury in 1836 after 300 years. Sir Stephen Glynne, brother-in-law of Gladstone, described St. Rumbold's as a 'small mean building ... having the battlements most absurdly painted white': it was the first to be rebuilt in 1840. Holy Trinity was the next to go, in spite of some opposition by parishioners, not because they wished to preserve the historic building, but because of the expense. In 1841 it was replaced by one of the first churches by George Gilbert Scott, described somewhat unflatteringly by a contemporary as a designer of workhouses. It was a very large church, its big windows filled with stained glass that included the arms of the Marquis of Westminster, the town and Bishop Dennison. It now became the towns' main church, but fortunately plans for demolishing St. Peter's and using its stone for this new building were not implemented.

The dissenting chapels also needed frequent rebuilding and enlargement with funds that seem to have been readily raised by their energetic members. The Independent or Congregational chapel was rebuilt in 1859 with 'an improved heating apparatus'; the handsome bath stone facade looks best viewed from the top of St. Peter's. The Methodist chapel in which Wesley preached was rebuilt in 1827, also

Harry Gatehouse, the saddler who appears in a later illustration outside his shop, seen here in Masonic dress.

in the classical style so often adopted by dissenters, repaired in 1864, but again replaced by the present Arts & Crafts Gothic building in 1907.

A movement that was connected with religon and seems to have become almost a religion in its own right was temperance. As tea and coffee became popular, then with increased production cheaper so that even the poor could drink them, it was possible for beer to be 'outlawed'. Temperance meetings and teas to which children could be taken provided some social life for wives. However I doubt if this movement had much effect on the cheerful regulars of Shaftesbury's still numerous pubs. A coal man called George Thick was told by the manager of the Gas Works: 'Your nose is very red George, you must be drinking rather heavy', to be quickly answered 'My nose is like your gas meters, registers more than it consumes'. Like the various sects, the Temperance movement has left its mark on Shaftesbury in the shape of the Temperance Hall in Bell Street, built in 1877. Later this changed from being the refuge of wives to a sanctuary for men: the Shaftesbury Masonic Lodge.

Universal education in England lagged behind the rest of the western world because the various sects could not agree to use the same schools. In Shaftesbury the Free School had disappeared and the twenty boys at Lush's Blue Coat School, an Anglican foundation, were the only children receiving a free education, excepting any bright enough to pick one up at the early Sunday schools, which aimed to teach children to read, but not usually to write. Parents able to pay for their children's education would either have employed a governess or tutor at home, or sent them to private day or boarding schools, usually run in the teacher's home. In an 1823 directory under 'Academies' Shaftesbury had four 'Gents' schools and the Misses Bacon ran a 'Ladies Boarding' school. The school-master at Lush's school was also allowed to take in a few paying pupils to supplement his salary.

The Rev. Thomas Evans, owner of the Grosvenor House Academy in Bleke Street, one of the private schools for boys that appeared in this directory, was an unlikely champion of education for the work-ing classes, but he was also the Congregational minister. In 1836 he opened a two-roomed 'British' school in Mustons Lane (next to the chapel and now a house). He was at pains to explain that the new school was for all sects, the children going to whatever place of worship their parents preferred on Sundays.

Although from 1833 both British and National (Anglican) schools received government grants, these did not cover costs and even with funds raised by 'fetes' and 'bazaars', a way rather similar to that being resorted to today, parents still had to pay. Evans did his best for large poor families by offering a bulk rate: three or more children from one family for 6d a week, the price of two. For girls, whose education was considered less important than boys, he offered the incentive that they would be taught needlework and knitting in addi-

Another of John Rutter's many ventures was this school in St. James, 'the poorest and most populous district of the Town'. It was typical of John Rutter that the school had a 'Soup House'. He lived in nearby 'Layton Cottage' and, although not poor himself, knew the problems of his neighbours.

The opening of the 1910 Wesleyan Bazaar in the lower Market Hall in the High Street. Not so very different to our present day fund raising 'dos', even to the man on the far left who hasn't managed to find the right stall for a large jar of pickled onions.

tion to the three R's. He also suggested in a footnote to his brochure that benevolent ladies could encourage poor but deserving families by paying for the girls education and 'have all their plain needlework done – give ease to the anguish of a mother's heart – afford little girls an honourable means of support, and secure them from poverty, vice and ruin' – all for 3d a week! By the time of the first public examination of the pupils six months later, the school had 101 boys and only 75 girls (possibly there was a shortage of benevolent ladies?).

Sadly, one of Thomas Evans boys at Grosvenor House School committed suicide and, although he, his wife and the school ushers were cleared of all blame, he gave up his school and his wife

Mrs. Evans girls school (now an architects office on the corner of Bleke Street) later became the Girls High School and looks idyllic in this Edwardian photograph.

A poster advertising the 'Morning Star' coach which ran between Shaftesbury and Salisbury to connect with trains that were by 1856 running between Salisbury and London.

Cheap Conveyance
TO AND FROM
Shaftesbury & London.

The Public are respectfully informed, that a

LIGHT SPRING VAN,
CALLED
"The Morning Star"

Will, on and after TUESDAY, the 8th of MAY, 1855,

Leave the King's Arms Inn, SHAFTESBURY, every *Tuesday, Thursday,* and *Saturday,* at half-past 5 o'clock in the morning, for the conveyance of Passengers & Luggage, and arrive in SALISBURY in time for the half-past 10 o'clock 1st, 2nd, & 3rd Class Train to SOUTHAMPTON, PORTSMOUTH, & LONDON; and will leave the Wheat Sheaf Inn, SALISBURY, for SHAFTESBURY, in the afternoon of the same days, immediately on the arrival of the 10-minutes-past-2 Train from LONDON.

FARES.
	s.	*d.*
To or from Shaftesbury & London, (3rd Class)	10	2
To or from Shaftesbury and Salisbury	3	0

converted Grosvenor House into a girls school.

In 1846 Earl Grosvenor gave the land for the National school in Abbey Walk and other National schools were built for the children of St. James, Cann and Enmore Green.

As the railway age dawned Shaftesbury was a thriving town containing enough shops and craftsmen to supply nearly every need of the townspeople and the farming area within a ten mile radius. On a market day in January 1836 Mr. Cundy, the South Western Railway engineer, came to the Grosvenor Arms to explain his Company's plans for a railway from London to Exeter via Salisbury. He received enthusiastic support from John Rutter who was soon busy calculating how cheaply coal could be brought to Shaftesbury if a line connected it to the Somerset coalfield, fuel being the most expensive commodity in the town.

By 1838 the railway had reached Basingstoke, but stage coaches still ran from there to Exeter for more than ten years, giving Shaftesbury's coaching trade a reprieve. It was therefore along the ancient Great West Road that the penny post was inaugurated in 1840. Ten years after the first railway meeting John Rutter was still campaigning for a line to go through from Salisbury to Exeter and at a meeting in Sherborne told the audience that 'they were living in 1846, but many noblemen still required to be reminded that their interests and conveniences must give way to the interests of the public'. In 1860 the railway was open from Salisbury to Exeter, but came no nearer than Semley. John Rutter never saw it as he died in 1851.

Between 1820 and 1919 Shaftesbury was something it had never been in its long history: a place with a ruling family. The rule appears to have been largely benevolent after the election quarrels of the early years and the town possibly received back in buildings and trade as much as tenants paid into the Westminster estates. Although everything was managed by agents, usually local solicitors, the Marquis of Westminster was not an absentee landlord and the family regularly stayed at Motcombe House.

When imported wheat began to undermine the farming economy towards the end of the century the patronage of rich landowners proved valuable. They came to their country estates for entertainment and for that purpose preserved game, kept horses and packs of hounds. The presence of the 'gentry' attracted others who could afford to choose where they lived, and all helped to support a wide range of good class shops which gave employment not only in the shops, but also to craftsmen in the town.

The benevolence of the Marquis of Westminster is apparent from a letter written to him by John Rutter in 1849 and by his response. Rutter had been asked for his suggestions for improvements the town needed and among his suggestions were a market house and a water supply for the poor. Lord Westminster, perhaps thinking of it as a memorial to his old adversary, in 1852 sank a 125 feet well with steam pumps at Barton Hill to provide water, not only free to the poor, but to everyone in the town.

In 1839 landowners near Shaftesbury formed an 'Association for the Protection of Persons and Property and Prosecution of Offenders' which met at the Grosvenor Arms annually and offered rewards for the capture of criminals. The surviving minute books record an unsatisfactory state of affairs with people, including Earl Grosvenor, so desperate to protect things like gardens, livestock and fences that they were willing to offer sizeable rewards and see terribly heavy sentences, including transportation, passed on poor wretches who were often stealing to live. For instance Elizabeth

Most of Earl Grosvenor's early building was in greensand from his own quarries, but he also had a brickworks at Motcombe and the bright red bricks and floor tiles stamped 'W' were used all over the town. He built houses as grand as Barton Hill House for wealthy tenants and solid cottages which carry this wheatsheaf badge.

Early photographs of Shaftesbury usually include urchins and working men, but the urchins always have boots and the men look as if they have work. The shops look very smart, note the carved and gilded fascia of this grocer at the corner of Bimport, and there are often elegant carriages like this one waiting outside the Literary Institute.

I am not sure exactly when this was taken, but the hunt would have been a familiar sight in Shaftesbury until 1939. Alfred Fricker has come out of his 'Grosvenor Cyclists' Home' in Salisbury Street to watch it pass. The pavements are clean, but the state of the road explains the need for watering in the summer.

Mr. Gatehouse standing outside his saddlery shop in Bell Street. His business prospered by providing both luxury items like the hunting saddle in the doorway and ordinary harness for working horses. At the corner of Parsons Pool the classical Wesleyan chapel is still standing, so the photograph must have been taken before 1907.

Chubb stole hay and a hurdle for which she was sentenced to a year's hard labour.

It was not only in Shaftesbury that such things were happening and it became clear that a more efficient force than town constables was needed in a country beginning to be linked by railways. The first workhouse board of guardians had been consulted about the formation of a police force in the 1830's, but it was not until 1855 that a county constabulary was established in Dorset. In spite of the usual doubts about any new system the police soon acquired a good reputation and the local 'bobby' usually became a liked and respected local figure.

The official notebook of PC 89 survives. He was sent to Shaftesbury in 1884, but as there is no name in the book nothing more can be discovered about him. Among his first duties was retrieving the body of a suicide victim from a pond in St. James. PC 89's regular work was rarely that dramatic: it comprised inspecting pubs (always 'no complaint'), meeting trains at Semley, pursuing workhouse escapees and duty at various public occasions from furniture sales to temperance rallies, once even in plain clothes.

He received instructions from his superintendant regarding crimes all over the country and invariably filled in 'making enquiries', usually followed by 'but no clue'. The crime detection rate in Shaftesbury however was high. The drunk and disorderly, the thieves of ducks and even the gentleman recorded as 'driving furious (sic) in the Commons' were apprehended, soon tried and marched to jail. The incredible thing is the mileage column of PC 89's report sheet. He regularly marched prisoners to Blandford and Sturminster on their way to jail at Dorchester and in his 7 day week walked as

In 1886 Mark Hanbury Beaufoy, whose family business was vinegar manufacture in Bermondsey, built himself a country house near Shaftesbury called 'Coombe House'. Like the Grosvenors the family brought employment and trade to the town. These festivities for the coming of age of his eldest son were entirely catered for by local firms.

much as 126 miles. No wonder a manufacturer in the town thought he might be able to interest the police in his 'Dorset Flyer' bicycle. No wonder also that almost PC 89's only time off during the year was 16 days spent sick with 'lumbago'.

After 1816 the Abbey ruins were ignored until the newly formed Wiltshire Archaeological Society decided to hold their summer meeting at Shaftesbury in 1861. The Marquis of Westminster paid for an excavation, but after the 70 or 80 ladies and gentlemen of the Society had examined the ruins, enjoyed the 'fat buck' provided at the 'Grosvenor Arms' by the Marquis and gone home, the foundations were filled in 'with proper reverence and respect' and largely forgotten again. In 1902 the second major excavation was undertaken by architect Edward Doran Webb, the site now belonging to Lord Westminster's son Lord Stalbridge, who had leased it to the Corporation. As usual with town affairs the dig started off with great pomp, the town band leading a procession to the site where ' Lord Stalbridge drove in the first iron bar'. Six feet of earth was removed and dumped all over the place, everyone came to look at the excavations and Doran Webb was made the first freeman of Shaftesbury, but in 1910 the town's interest had waned and he was asked to remove the excavation finds from the Town Hall.

The Marquis of Westminster died in 1869, but his wife and daughter retained their connections with Shaftesbury and commemorated him by giving the Westminster Memorial Hospital to the town in 1871. Cottage hospitals were a means by which the rich could donate money to help the poor, but the donors liked to make sure that their money was not spent on the undeserving poor, so for each £20 or annual subscription of one guinea the subscriber was allowed to nominate one patient for a month. The patient had to pay

The original Westminster Memorial Hospital of 1871. The handsome building, on one of the finest sites in the town, still forms the core of a hospital that continues to serve the people of Shaftesbury.

The decorations for Lady Theodora Grosvenor's wedding to Ivor Guest from Canford in 1874. Her father's Market Hall entrance is to the left of the picture and the Wiltshire & Dorset Bank, with its original ground floor, next on the right.

The Marquis of Westminster's daughter Theodora was particularly fond of Shaftesbury and their Motcombe home.

Although after 1852 Shaftesbury was adequately supplied with water, the outside taps easily froze up. Peach's the barbers were the only people in Salisbury Street with water during February and March 1895 and kept their neighbours supplied. Note the yokes and milk churns, then readily available.

A High School reunion in 1905.

This is said to be 'Bristol George' (George Gatehouse), in which case the smart carriage is not a private one, as he combined being market clerk on Saturdays with carriage hire. It is standing in Bell Street and the scene is little changed except that the brick facade of No. 36 is now rendered.

upwards of 2/- a week, and other rules excluded people who could not guarantee the cost of their removal or burial, people with infectious diseases or incurable conditions and 'cases of maternity', but cases of 'urgency or severe accident' were admitted at any time. The patient was allowed visitors only on Sundays and Thursdays, only reading matter approved by the Chaplain, and had to help clean the ward and feed other patients when able.

In 1871 the first wholesale milk depot to collect milk for the increasing needs of London was opened at Semley station. The problem of collecting warm milk from farms and transporting it to London for distribution the next day was solved by advances in chilling techniques so that by 1882 twice daily despatches of chilled milk were leaving Semley for London. The area fairly rapidly changed from being mainly concerned with butter and cheese-making to bulk milk supply. There was perhaps less work on the farms, but the pace of life increased as more cows were milked and the milk taken in churns to the depot by horse and cart to be ready for the next train. Local tinsmiths had to learn to make the new churns designed for railway transport, while harness makers and blacksmith's work had more urgency if failure to get the milk to the depot resulted in the waste of a whole day's production on the farm.

In Thomas Hardy's *Jude the Obscure* the controversial scene where the young schoolmistress leaves her schoolmaster husband is set in Bimport. Ox House was their gloomy home, their school the National School opposite. Not only did Hardy use Shaston, the abbreviation that had been Shaftesbury's common name for cen-

E.F. Hooper had a large drapery shop in No. 51 & 53 High Street in the 1880's and a photographic studio at No. 58 opposite. The 'Rummage Sale' was being held in the back yard of No. 58 as the thatched roofs of Angel Lane can be seen in the background. After Hooper died his widow married his manager, Albert Upfield, (standing in front of the sale posters) who continued both the drapery and photography businesses.

The toll house that stood at the junction of the Salisbury and Ringwood roads near the 'Half Moon'. The Weldon family, who took hand-powered roundabouts and swing boats to fairs, lived there at the turn of the century. Donna Weldon was famous for her gingerbread.

The Commons in 1900. George Imber's butcher's shop is between the 'Grosvenor' and Pearson the printer. George Elsey patented his own bread mixer and his bakery was in the basement below his cafe.

'Omnibuses' outside the Grosvenor in about 1890 give the impression that stage coaches still ran on the Great West Road, but these old vehicles were to take passengers to and from Semley station, although it was locally held that a brisk walk up Semley Hollow got you to Shaftesbury more quickly and saved 1/-. A carrier's cart can be seen on the left, these continued to carry people and goods between villages and market towns until the arrival of motor buses.

No. 27 High Street at the turn of the century. The skilful display extending out onto the pavement includes some items a similar shop might sell today. But the large crocks, priced at from 7/-, probably came from Verwood and would have been used to store water overnight, when the town supply was usually turned off.

Phillip Short's wheelwrights and coachbuilding business was where the Post Office now stands. This photograph was probably taken on market day around 1900, when the firm still sold vehicles such as the elegant high wheeled gentlemans gig, hand-made by the men and apprentices lined up for their photograph. But the petrol signs presage things to come as traffic along the old Great West Road began to increase again and the building on the site of the Angel Inn became a garage.

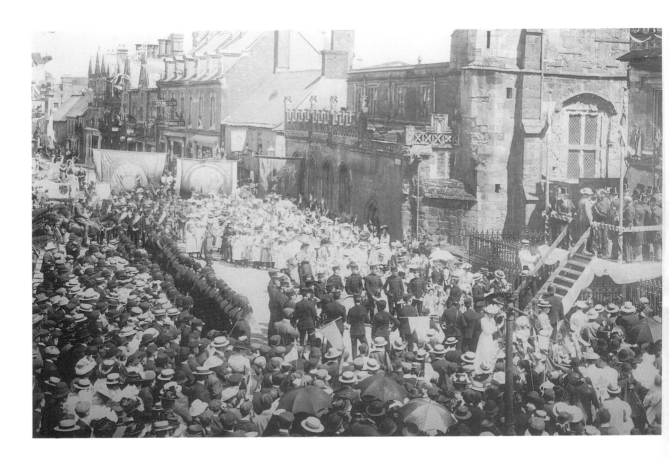

Watches being presented to returned Boer War soldiers outside the Town Hall. The watches were made by Frederick Woodcock of Angel Square and the Museum has the one presented to Private E.T.B. Alford.

turies, instead of his usual made-up name, but he wrote as if he knew Shaftesbury well in the 1880's. He describes it as: 'the resting place and headquarters of the proprietors of wandering vans, shows, shooting galleries, and other itinerate concerns, whose business lay largely at fairs and markets. As strange wild birds are seen assembled on some lofty promontory, meditatively pausing for longer flights, or to return to the course they followed thither, so here, in the cliff-town stood in stultified silence the yellow and green caravans bearing names not local, as if surprised by a change in the landscape so violent as to hinder their further progress; and here they usually remained all the winter till they turned to seek again their old tracks in the following spring.' This is particularly interesting as several Shastonians who knew the town when Hardy did mention fairground people who lived locally.

William Farley Rutter, solicitor grandson of John Rutter, described the fair at St. Martin's as a 'very lively affair. On the Saturday there would be swing boats in the street in front of St. Peter's Church so that those who went aboard would swing up and over the parapet of the church aisle. There would be a shooting gallery and coconut shies in front of the Town Hall and probably a tent exhibiting a fat woman or a steam roundabout in the corner. Then there were stalls, selling a variety of things, up the High Street in front of the shops

92

Shaftesbury's 1907 historical tableaux was organized to raise money to add a chancel to Holy Trinity. It was held in the Market Hall, although this picture of 'The Byzant Dance' was taken outdoors. All the town was involved, many people such as the macebearers and mayor (Dr Harris), playing themselves.

Shaftesbury VAD's posed in a High Street garden at the beginning of the First World War.

and the 'Grosvenor Hotel' and on the Commons. The readers must understand that when people who flocked into the town from the country round were added to the local population the whole street was fairly choc a bloc with people, and traffic such as there was, had difficulty in getting through.' All this of course was on the Great West Road!

Although, like Hardy, he was fascinated with the romantic past, the surgeon turned writer Sir Frederick Treves did not see Shaftesbury as, 'world forgotten', but 'bright, pleasant and healthy'. Gradually the first trickle of visitors began to come to see 'headlong'

An army bi-plane that fell on the Grammar School playing field in 1916. There appears to be an army camp in the distance and the fragile aircraft may have intended to land on the pitches.

Gold Hill and the Abbey wall with its 'enormous straining buttresses . . . the shoulders of each leaning back with fearful effort towards the line of houses on the ridge . . . holding up the town with might and main.' Victorian holidaymakers and intending residents were usually advised to check up on the drains, which may account for the Corporation setting up a sewage farm at Holyrood in the 1890's. This was a sewage farm in the original meaning of the term: raw sewage was run onto the fields where the grass provided a fairly adequate treatment – and especially good pasture.

Although war had not touched Shaftesbury for centuries, soldiers were probably more in evidence than they are now. In 1874 a unit of the 9th Dorset Rifle Volunteers were based at the Armoury in Bell Street (now No. 45) under the command of Shaftesbury's MP Vere Fane-Benett-Stanford. Cannon from the Crimea War adorned Park Walk and old soldiers, who lived at the doss houses on Gold Hill, could collect a few coppers by performing gun drill when citizens were promenading on Park Walk. When World War I commenced soldiers were billeted in the town and the drill on the Park was in earnest. The 136 Shastonians who lost their lives in the war are commemorated on war memorials in Park Walk, St. James, Cann and Enmore Green. One Shastonian who did return was Charles King, but he later died of wounds in a Sunderland hospital. His wife had to leave their two small children to go up and arrange for him to be buried in Holy Trinity churchyard.

Independent Shaftesbury
1918-1992

The Sale of Shaftesbury in 1918-1919 was a similar turning point in the history of the town to the closure of the Abbey 380 years earlier. Again there had been indications of change, and the decision to sell by the second Lord Stalbridge, who had inherited the Shaftesbury and Stalbridge properties from his father in 1912, did not come as a complete surprise. Even before World War I landowners in the area had been selling off parts of their estates, indeed the first Lord Stalbridge had already sold some of his property in Shaftesbury.

Before the auction announced by Knight, Frank & Rutley for September 1918 could take place the whole of Shaftesbury was bought by James White and two other Londoners for £75,000. Under Lord Stalbridge's covenant the town was then offered to the Mayor and Corporation who decided it was impossible for the Borough to purchase it, even at a 'reasonable price'. A 'Ratepayer' suggested that the town might ask James White if they could buy the public utilities (waterworks, cattle market, etc.,), but the idea was dismissed without even asking White.

Only four days after this meeting Dr.Harris, Robert Borley and Herbert Viney purchased the entire town from James White and his partners for £80,000. Ordinary tenants were probably relieved to know that their homes were now in the hands of local men. Dr. Harris, who lived at 'Avishays', (now Abbeyfield's 'Pepperill House') and had his surgery in what is now 'The Ship' next door, was a kindly man who took small convalescent boys for rides in his pony and trap or red motor car when making his rounds. He also went out to attend the confinements of gipsy women, a particular kindness as the hated alternative if they needed medical attention was having their babies in the Workhouse. Equally well known, but probably not so popular, was Robert Borley the innkeeper, who had been Mayor in 1899, 1904 and 1907. The third member of the 'Syndicate' was Herbert Viney, manager of the largest firm in the town. Stratton, Sons & Mead was a wholesale and retail grocers with a large shop where No. 36 High Street is now and a mineral water factory at the water works. They also supplied village shops as far away as Bruton and sent local eggs and cheese up to London stores, including William Whiteleys and Selfridges. Fred Long, an employee for 45 years, described Herbert Viney as a 'very shrewd businessman'.

Before the Syndicate's auction of the Town in over 300 separate lots a Tenants Association was formed comprising nearly all the people affected, who agreed to bid for their own premises and not for those of other members – unless that member had already dropped out of the bidding. When the long-anticipated sale took place on 27-29th May 1919 in the Lower Market Hall it must have been an exciting experience for all, and a frightening one for some. Most people were able to buy their premises, particularly the moderately well-off. Those least able to bid were the cottagers, particularly widows, but it was rare for the poor to be home owners in 1919.

On the second afternoon four pubs and most of the High Street shops were auctioned, with the audience applauding when popular shopkeepers acquired their premises. One who was outbid was the butcher George Imber whose shop at 9 High Street went to an outsider for £1,950. By some means the Vendors persuaded the buyer to withdraw and Mr. Imber ended up buying his shop for only £1,500. William Farley Rutter, son of the Town Clerk John Kingsley Rutter and great grandson of John Rutter, thanked the Syndicate on behalf of the Tenants Association and asked if something could be done for Andrew Gower, the wine merchant at No. 38 High Street, who had also been an unsuccessful bidder, but was told 'the premises were large ones and Mr. Gower did not go very far in the matter of bidding'.

The auctioneer, William Fox of Bournemouth, was a skilful showman and kept interest up by such announcements as 'Albert Dean, grocer and well known political agent, has occupied this house for no less than 72 years'. After buying his house and shop, No. 59 St. James Street, Albert told *The Western Gazette* that he had been born in his present bedroom and intended to sleep there until carried out 'on his last earthly journey'. Although described as a grocer Albert was most renowned for his pork, the pigs being slaughtered in the yard at the back.

The auctioneer's prediction that after the sale 'there would be a different spirit in the place' with 300 owners instead of one was correct. The Tenants Association became 'The Borough Welfare Association', with the intention primarily of wresting control of the town's water supply which had been retained by the Syndicate. In a town where water had been free for as long as most people could remember the thought of paying for it must have been unwelcome, and with a total monopoly the Syndicate could charge what it liked.

The Corporation had bought the fire station, market house, cattle market, cricket ground and allotments in Coppice Street to be used for housing. The Syndicate had given the Park to the town and Dr. Harris had arranged for Castle Hill to be a permanent open space, but they had made a substantial profit on their investment and it was feared that they intended to add to their income at the expense of the townspeople by retaining the Water Works and favoured building sites such as the Abbey ruins.

The Borough Welfare Association had seven other stated aims. To improve drainage and sanitation: even some central parts of the town were without sewers. To find a new burial ground: St. Peter's

GATEHOUSE

Elections, even after things had quietened down from the violence of the 19th century, were never tame affairs in Shaftesbury as can be seen from this sea of excited faces waiting for the announcement of election results by the mayor in the 1920's.

had no churchyard, and that of Holy Trinity had much earlier been reported to be in an unhealthily overcrowded state and the other churches had little or no land. To commemorate the men who died in the Great War and reward the survivors: some thought sports grounds were better than crosses others, including the returning soldiers, preferred 'Homes Fit for Heroes' – the 'Welfarists' were intent on providing all three. To ensure that allotments remained available: formerly Lord Stalbridge had let them cheaply to working men to grow potatoes and vegetables. The land being purchased by the Borough for 'council' houses was allotments and it was feared that in the free market created by the sale the rents of the others would go beyond the pockets of those who most needed them, even if all the sites that had been described in the auction catalogue as 'ripe for development' were not built on. As their programme demanded so much land and the town had little left the Association's final proposal was the extension of the Borough boundaries, which would have the added benefit of enabling them to take advantage of larger government loans.

In the 1919 Borough Council election, described by participant Farley Rutter as 'one of the most exciting in the history of the Borough', the four 'Welfarist' candidates were elected and in the following year, after another no holds barred election, four more got in. Some 'Welfarists' were people dissatisfied with the Sale. Dr. Harold Utterton Gould MB was a fox hunting doctor who had leased Castle Hill House in 1907 for 21 years, but had been unable to buy it when the Syndicate bid £2,100 and had to move to far less spacious surroundings in what is now 'King Alfred's Kitchen'. Another member was F. Coaker, a blind man with a shop at No. 25 High Street, who to earn a living as a piano tuner 'used to ride a tandem with a sighted man in front, sometimes as far as Poole.' Mr. Coaker had bought his premises with his first bid, according to Dr. Harris 'in view of his affliction', but accused the Syndicate of being the 'most collosal profiteers'.

Charles R. Dickenson had been a member of the Tenants Association, but had bought 18 properties in the sale, none of them apparently his own home and more than half belonging to poor widows, also some allotments. He, of course, faced a high rates bill if the improvements demanded by the reforming 'Welfarists' were implemented, so stood as a Borough Council candidate for the 'Borleyites'.

After all this excitement the town settled down to a changed way of life. For some, such as the spinster who found her new landlord charged £13 a year for her cottage instead of the £5.10.0 she had paid Lord Stalbridge, it must have been harder. However the War Memorials were built, a cemetery was opened in Mampitts Lane in 1927, council houses went up slowly in Coppice Street and Old Boundary Road and the men who had returned from the War played cricket on a pitch now owned by the town. After an expensive legal battle the town had obtained the waterworks, and economically turned a redundant water storage tank into a swimming bath (which is still in use). The drought of 1921 raised doubts about the supply at Barton Hill, but other sources at Wincombe Park and elsewhere did not prove necessary. The sewers were gradually extended, necessitating another 'farm' at Paynes Place Farm for the disposal of effluent.

Another municipal service we cannot imagine ever having been without was instituted in the 1920's. Frank Brockway who lived in St. James with his brother Charles from Enmore Green, general hauliers, were paid the princely sum of £1 per week to remove house refuse, which they agreed to do so long as they also got the contract for watering the streets to lay the dust. Refuse was tipped into various holes around the Borough including Boyn Mead stone quarry, pits at Motcombe Brick Works and Mampitts Lane and the 'old quarry, Salisbury Road'. Street watering had been necessary on the rough stone roads before the coming of the car demanded 'surface painting'.

In doing his best to help a returning soldier one local landlord came upon a long-hidden piece of Abbey property. Ernest Johnson had agreed to let No. 50 High Street to a baker and feeling that the old fireplace was dilapidated told his workmen to replace it. Behind it they discovered the fourteenth century alabaster carving now in the Shaftesbury History Society Museum.

Robert Borley retained the Abbey site after the sale and it was sold to the Claridges in the 1930's. They opened it to the public and

ontinued excavating, finding the contentious 'bones' which were
nought to be those of King Edward the Martyr.

The hospital had received its last gift from the Westminsters in
907 when Lady Theodora Guest presented an operating room in
nemory of her mother, after that large donations came mainly from
roups such as the Carnival Committee or the Farmers Club. The
ospital was getting bigger and more complicated, for instance X ray
quipment was installed in 1919 with money raised by the Car-
ival, which all added to running costs. In 1923 no carnival was
eld, apparently because the Hospital Management Committee had
efused to sack the Matron who was disliked by the Carnival
ommittee. This left the Hospital short of funds and when the
Matron resigned the Hospital was closed for nearly two months. In
928 a Hospital League was formed which operated as a form of
ealth insurance by which townspeople paid in regular contributions
meet the expense of running the hospital and in return received
ee treatment. In 1938 hospital grouping began and the Committee
ecided they wished Shaftesbury to join the Salisbury group: to
hich it still belongs.

Farley Rutter describing the twenties and thirties says unemploy-
ent was not a particular problem in Shaftesbury, also that out-
-work miners from South Wales came to here to dig the new
wers. Certainly there is evidence that local builders not only found

For the 1935 'Silver Jubilee'
Mayor Robert Borley decided
that 'whatever the vegetarians
said' an Ox Roast, such as he had
organized when he was mayor in
1910, would provide 'something
for the children to remember'.

Farris' Belle Vue Ironworks, which stood where 'Homefarris House' is now, was almost Shaftesbury's only heavy industry and employed as many as 80 men in its heyday. It hired out 'steam rollers' for road surfacing as well as supplying farmers in a wide area with steam equipment for threshing and other farm work.

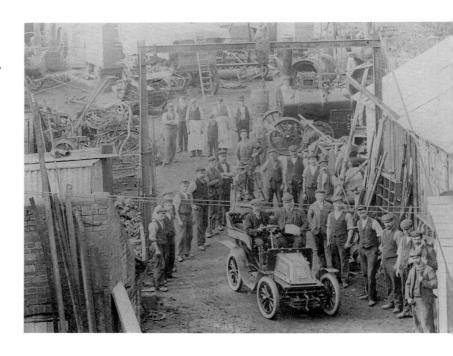

employment constructing 'council' houses, but also worked on a limited number of private houses. There were no slums to clear in Shaftesbury: most of 'Poor Yard' had gone, although two of the cottages survived until replaced by Council houses in the 1950's.

With the modernization of services in the town it is strange to come across a letter written by the Town Clerk in 1920 informing watchmaker George Hillier that he has been appointed 'Winder of clocks at the Town Hall and Curfew bell ringer on the same terms as Mr. Woodcock, viz £10 a year.' George's daughter took up these ancient duties after him, and actually rang the curfew for a short time after World War II.

In at least one Shaftesbury house the pre-war style of life continued. Castle Hill House was bought in the 1920's by Isaac Bell, a wealthy American who was like 'an English character out of Surtees'. After only two terms at Cambridge he decided to become an MFH rather than an MA. Once Master of the South West Wiltshire Foxhounds 'Ikey' moved to Shaftesbury where he kept 45 hunters and ran a Rolls Royce, providing both employment and entertainment in the town until 1940 when he went to Ireland and became MFH to the Galway Blazers. Parts of the present Health Centre are the stables added by him to Castle Hill House.

Farris' first car mechanic, Reg Stevens, was also the part owner with a grocer in Hindon of two red charabancs that provided an early motorbus service. Some of the ironwork supplied by Farris' Belle Vue Ironworks for drainage schemes can still be seen around the town. Farris' were also the first firm in the town to have electric light, run from their own generator.

In 1929 the Wessex Electricity Company established an office in Bell Street (now No.28) with a staff of four, including a local girl to type letters and run the showroom and Mr. W.J. Purnell, who still lives in Shaftesbury, as second engineer. The Shaftesbury Gas & Coke Company was still tendering for street lighting when the new council houses were built in 1932, but in 1931 the Town Hall was converted to electricity and in 1935 street lighting became electric. But Shaftesbury was not particularly backward, even London suburbs did not all convert to electric street lighting until after World War II. Shaftesbury's last remaining gas standards were being removed in 1946, imitation ones are being put up today!

The development of cars, lorries and buses in the twenties and thirties put Shaftesbury back on the map on the main route from London to Cornwall and, as cars became a reliable all-weather form of transport people who could afford this luxury took motoring holidays and even started to buy houses in the country. Large houses such as 'Coombe House' and 'Belmont House' became 'Country House Hotels', the 'Grosvenor Arms' entered a new phase as a 'Trust House' and 'artistic' people settled around Shaftesbury.

One artist who was drawn to the area was the 21-year-old Cecil Beaton who, having fallen in love with some derelict eighteenth century stables hidden in a valley near Win Green, found himself with Robert Borley as his landlord: the retired innkeeper owned the woodland and used the buildings for his pheasants. A more disparate landlord and tenant would be hard to imagine. Beaton had been warned of Borley's 'ferocity' and described him as a 'large and prosperous elderly man without much imagination, but a sound

A cartoon of the fire brigade showing them 'about to set out on a fire-extinguishing expedition, within three or four hours of being called!' It is amazing to think of Shaftesbury in the 1920's still having a volunteer fire brigade called out by boys and pulling the engine to the fire themselves if horses could not be found (reputedly as far as Tisbury). In 1927 a fire at the Grosvenor jolted Shaftesbury into the 20th century and a motor engine was bought.

Amongst the artistic people attracted to Shaftesbury between the wars were Mr and Mrs James Masters, who lived quietly in the centre of the town at 'High House' and produced fine printing, such as this picture of the High Street from their upstairs window.

The war had its lighter moments, especially for children – as this Home Guard demonstration shows.

practical sense'; goodness knows what Borley thought of him. Fo the next 15 years, while Cecil Beaton rented 'Ashcombe', rumours o the 'nudist colony' (only sunbathing actually, and far from nude with its visitors, who ranged from Rex Whistler to Augustus Joh and Salvador Dali, echoed round Shaftesbury.

The Town Clerk, Farley Rutter, together with the Mayor Ralp Pearson, remained in office for the duration of the Second Worl War. One of their many jobs was the local organization of rationing A list survives of grocers in the town who agreed to supply th rations of the registered customers of any other grocer who wa 'rendered unavailable for business directly or indirectly throug enemy action'. In those days there were 25 grocers in the Borough a well as butchers, greengrocers and other food shops. Fortunately fo Shaftesbury enemy action never closed any of Shaftesbury's shop and only one property in the Borough was even damaged: a bun galow at Ivy Cross which was hit by a crashing plane, but th inhabitants were unharmed. Nevertheless Shaftesbury was not on of those places which 'didn't know there was a war on', to quote favourite phrase of the time. It must have been uncomfortabl perched up here with enemy bombers flying over to bomb Bristo and the South Wales industrial areas, which gave rise to two alert from the siren on the top of the Town Hall each time. Shastonian must have feared that their town would share the fate of nearb Sherborne, which was bombed more heavily than many industria towns on a sunny afternoon in September 1940. Aware of the Wa while not directly suffering from it, Shastonians showed gratitud

Stories of bits of Dorset being 'knocked off by a tank' gain conviction when you see this photograph of D-Day equipment negotiating Angel Lane.

for their escape by giving generously to all kinds of collections.

One item Shaftesbury was not keen to contribute to the War effort was its iron railings. In September 1941 the Town Clerk and a retired engineer, Edwyn Jervoise, fired the first shot in the battle. The response from the owners of 'unneccessary iron railings' was immediate, from the widow who feared 'having derelict and open premises with so much loitering in the street' to the owner of 'Weighbridge House' who sent a neat sketch to explain how, if his railings were removed, in the blackout people would fall over the remaining stone wall 'with the possibility of hitting their heads on the bay window'. Opposite, the owner of 'Bimport House' thought that without his railings people would fall into his garden as 'hundreds of people queue up for the cinema in the dark'. Nearly everyone mentioned that their railings were necessary to keep out cattle, a reminder that they were still driven through Shaftesbury streets 'in twos and elevens', as Albert Burden put it. Stanley Farris wrote that the railings at 'Llanreath House' would make less than '2 cwts of good steel' and pointed out that the Ministry had not collected the 10-12 tons of scrap steel that his father had offered. Only the railings of 'Manor House', St. James, were reprieved by the architect who came from Yeovil, as they dated from before 1820. But Shaftesbury retained all its railings in the end as the Ministry of Supply stopped collecting them in September 1944, just before the contractor from Southampton was due to come up for them.

Even while the War was still on national plans were drawn up for drastic changes in education and public health, which were implemented soon after it finished. In Shaftesbury the two fee-paying schools, the Boys Grammar School and the Girls High School, became free to local boys or girls who passed the '11 plus' examination and for those who did not a new mixed Secondary Modern

School was built in Mampitts Lane. This seems to have freed enough space in the old National schools to accommodate the increasing numbers of younger children.

The birthrate went up steeply after the War, and even the Westminster Memorial Hospital had an increase from 14 births in 1940 to 112 in 1945, therefore the Hospital took steps to cope by acquiring 'Castle Hill House' for a separate maternity unit. The increase was partly due to the rise in the birthrate, partly to the new belief that it was safer for mothers and babies if births took place in hospital. In 1948, with the introduction of the National Health Service, 74 years of financing Shaftesbury's local hospital by patients' fees, private donations and such things as carnival collections ceased, and all medical treatment, as well as all education, became free to everyone who needed it. The 'Friends of the Hospital' then turned their attention to raising money for extra comforts such as radios and a day room for the patients.

At about this time the last vestiges of the old Poor Law disappeared. The main purpose of workhouses had gone with the introduction of pensions and unemployment pay. 'Alcester House' was still in use for its secondary purpose of providing shelter for the sick poor and in 1949, when Dorset County Council proposed to close it, the Hospital Management Committee campaigned unsuccessfully to retain it as a 40 bed unit to house the chronically sick. In spite of dramatic protests by Dr.Chapman, the Workhouse was demolished and eventually special wards were added to the Hospital enabling elderly Shastonians to be nursed near to their relations and friends.

In May 1946 the Shaftesbury & District Historical Society was formed. It was the inspiration of Noel Teulon Porter, a keen archaeologist who had retired to Shaftesbury from Cambridge. As in so many areas of Shaftesbury life, Farley Rutter did a great deal of work for it and was still Vice President when he died in 1991 aged 103. He said the idea originated when the road at the top of St. Johns Hill was widened and two shafts were found which baffled local archaeologists. Among the early members were eminent archaeologists, including Sir Leonard Woolley. Much excavating was done and very soon the Borough Council let them have the room at the Town Hall 'formerly used by the Billeting Officer' for a museum. With a rapidly expanding collection the museum moved to Gold Hill and, fortunately for the present Society, the members decided to buy 'Sun & Moon Cottage' when it came on the market in 1957. Their hours of hard work turned the old pub and doss house, on a site that has been occupied for about 800 years, into a good local museum.

In 1949 the Shaftesbury & District Arts Club was founded. The covered market had long ceased to be used for its original purpose and the High Street end had already been sold when, in 1951, the Borough decided to sell the Bell Street end. Once again a group of enthusiasts quickly made the right decision to buy their own headquarters and to undertake a lot of hard work to turn not very

suitable premises into a good theatre and exhibition centre. It opened in 1957 with *The Sleeping Monk*, written by Laura Sydenham, who since 1951 had been part-owner, with her friend Phyllis Carter, of the Abbey ruins. Takings from the ten day run contributed to funds being raised by another group of townspeople to repair St. Peter's church. The theatre was destroyed by a fire that started next door in 1965, but the members once again worked hard and within two years it was open again.

Shaftesbury's first new building after the war was the Post Office, which had been started before the war and finished in 1946. It is a handsome building, but the removal of cottages to build it spoiled a picturesque entrance to the town. Two listed buildings at the corner of Shooters Lane were replaced with 'contemporary' shops in the 1950's and a couple of good-looking shops were lost from the other side of the High Street, but in the mid 1960's a plan was produced that would have wiped out Shaftesbury as certainly as a concentrated air raid.

As far back as 1943 it was envisaged that Shaftesbury should develop to the east of Christy's Lane, but it was not until 1960 that the Borough bought land there for an egg-packing station and a laundry, also 125 acres more farmland was allocated for council housing and further factories. It was felt that these must be integrated with the town centre to the west and at the same time a solution to the problem of having two main roads looping through

This was a one-off revival of the Byzant ceremony in the 1960's. There is still a carnival and in the 1970's Gold Hill Fair was revived to raise funds for the repair of St. Peter's and has continued. The bowman at the head of this procession is Stanley Mansbridge, a great character who re-created the town's bellman or cryer.

the High Street and the Commons urgently needed to be found. In 1965 a Town Plan was exhibited at the Town Hall which, when the real intentions had been elucidated from the planner's jargon, must have come as a bit of a bombshell. Christy's Lane made the obvious route for by-passing the Town, and a bridge was to be built across it to allow people living in the new houses to drive into the centre. Two stacker car parks were to be built in the town and the one way road system necessitated a huge roundabout and road widening that would have destroyed most of Angel Lane and Haimes Lane. Most controversial of all was the proposal to demolish the south side of the High Street and build flats.

With only a week to consider these proposals Shastonians reacted quickly. The Civic Society was formed, Rolf Gardiner of Springhead, the environmentalist, came to the old town's defence and William Farley Rutter, by then nearly 80, protested about the secrecy and haste with which the proposals were submitted to the people of Shaftesbury. Because of the controversy this plan was dropped.

But worse was to come. During 1966 and 1967 the Borough Council, together with the Dorset County Council, were in negotiation with the Greater London Council to build an overspill town on the land east of Christy's Lane. This time there was more consultation with townspeople, who were told that Shaftesbury had to 'expand or die'. At the Public Inquiry at the Town Hall in 1968 the Civic Society presented an alternative plan. Rolf Gardiner, insisting he was an 'amateur', made valid objections on aesthetic grounds. Stephen Scammell, who had formed a protest group called 'Dorset in Danger' made some telling criticisms, and it may have been his reference to Andover that tipped the balance. It was known that problems were being encountered with the overspill town at Andover, and this perhaps made people see the flaws in the rosy pictures painted by the planners.

The overspill plan was dropped and fortunately calls at the Inquiry for the by-pass to be completed before any destructive road works were undertaken in the town seems to have been acted upon. These road works have not yet taken place and Shaftesbury, unlike Wimborne and many other towns, still has no one way traffic rushing through, so elderly people are still able to cross the High Street and walk through the lanes in the centre of the town in comparative peace. On the far side of Christy's Lane a new brick town has grown up, but it has developed gradually, with a pleasant mixture of houses, and people of all age groups, who have in common that they independently chose to come and live in Shaftesbury.

St. Peter's church was in a semi-redundant state for over a century, only used for occasional summer services as there was no lighting or heating and the roof leaked. Its salvation also took a long time. Eric Stevens was appointed architect in 1954 and devised a means of saving the main roof. Ominously, money for this came from the

Redundant Churches Fund, for it had been decided to abandon St. Peter's and make Holy Trinity the town's main church. But suddenly the long years of neglect of the building and argument about its value to Shaftesbury were ended by the discovery in 1973 that Holy Trinity, after little more than a century of use, needed structural repairs.

The decision in 1974 to de-consecrate Holy Trinity and make St. Peter's the main church was doubly lucky for Shaftesbury because St.Peter's now makes a beautifully light, modern church in a historic building, and the town landmark of Holy Trinity was retained with its ancient lime walks in the churchyard. Here excellent use has been made of the considerable interior space for a day centre, a gymnasium and other offices and headquarters for local groups. But the change of use of churches which have meant so much to people is rarely accomplished without pain to someone: Mrs. King, who had been so determined to have her young husband brought back to Holy Trinity churchyard half a century before, was faced with the removal of his grave when it was decided that the churchyard was to be levelled. Fortunately her daughters applied to the War Graves Commission and his grave is still marked by a headstone and fresh flowers. St. Rumbold's church at Cann also ceased to be a parish church in 1971, to the great sorrow of its remaining parishioners, but it became a school chapel to the boys Grammar School until that disappeared in 1983, and is now the Upper School Arts Centre.

The Day Centre at Holy Trinity is only part of a considerable organization for the care of Shastonians as they get old that has recently developed in the town. Both of Shaftesbury's ancient almshouses were re-built: Chubb's on exactly the same site, Spiller's as flats, while on part of the charities' land the more recent concept of 'Sheltered Housing' has been adopted in the form of particularly well-designed and laid out flats and houses. There are in addition to these old foundations, several other groups of flats in the centre of the town, which makes for a lively town centre as people walk to the shops and social events. The existence of more than 45 societies and groups tends to confirm that Shaftesbury did not die as predicted by the planners in 1968.

One of the first 'nostalgia' advertisements made in 1973 used Gold Hill as the setting for a 45-second television advertisement that has become one of the most famous ever shown. In 1982 Rank Hovis got further mileage out of their advertisement by finding the original boy, who had 'retired' from acting and become a fireman, and bringing him back to the Hill for the presentation of a £10,000 cheque towards the restoration of the cobbles. A large Hovis loaf still collects money for restoration work and if it is removed many visitors ask where it has gone. Another mild dissatisfaction expressed by visitors is that they 'thought it was Yorkshire', which is what the accents in the film implied, but generally people seem to enjoy what they find in Shaftesbury and themselves add pleasantly to the life and

The advertisement that everyone remembers.

trade of the town.

In 1974, when so many areas were losing their identity, Shaftesbury ceased to be what she had claimed to be 'time out of mind': a borough. Now merely part of North Dorset and shorn of her aldermen, the last of whose blue gowns now repose in the Museum, Shaftesbury retains her Mayor and Councillors who continue to campaign for improvements in the town in a continually changing world as the best of them did in the past.

The secondary modern school that was only built in the 1950's and the old Girl's High School, turned County Grammar School, became redundant in 1983 when comprehensive education was introduced. A Middle School was opened in Wincombe Lane and a new building on the Boy's Grammar School playing fields became the co-educational Upper School, keeping the long-standing tradition of both grammar schools of taking boarders.

Since 1970, in addition to new schools and many private houses on the east of Christy's Lane, there has been some infilling of houses and shops in the old town. Most of them have been distinct improvements, but some echoes of the devastating schemes of the 1960's remain: three cottages were demolished breaking the pleasant line of

The popular 'WI' market on Thursday mornings in the Town Hall in 1992.

Salisbury Street in 1986 and part of Coppice Street remains 'planning blighted', awaiting a one way system of doubtful usefulness. While in Victoria Street, on one of the sites proposed for stacker car parks, a row of well-built stables, that even in the 1919 sale were described as suitable for conversion into 7 cottages, still awaits demolition to provide a car park that will disrupt a quiet residential street.

The national revival of street markets and informal shopping in the 1960s found an echo in Shaftesbury with the opening of a Womens Institute market in the Town Hall in 1974. Supported by the open air market outside and a market for books, crafts and antiques in St. Peter's Hall, Thursday is now a real market day and generates a number of extra buses from the villages around. It is interesting to think that fish from Poole, eggs and chickens from local farms, produce of gardens in the town and even locally made goods are being sold on the very spot where they have been sold for at least 800 years, and people still come in from the surrounding area to this small market town, which has existed for so long, changing, but unchanged.

Bibliography

Adams, Thomas *A History of the Ancient Town of Shaftesbury* (1807)

Beaton, Cecil *Ashcombe: the Story of a Fifteen Year Lease* (1949)

Bettey, J.H. *City & County Histories Dorset* (1974)
  Landscape of Wessex (1980)
  Rural Life in Wessex 1500-1900 (1977)
  Suppression of the Monasteries in the West Country (1989)
  Wessex From A.D. 1000 (1986)

Biggs, Barry J. *The Wesleys and the Early Dorset Methodists* (1987)

Bowles, Charles(?) *Shaftesbury Corporation and Charities* (c. 1832)

Buchanan, Mary *Compton Abbas: A Dorset Village* (1991)

Clarendon, Edward, Earl of *History of the Rebellion & Civil Wars in England Begun in the Year 1641* (1703)

Cockburn, Elizabeth O. *The Almshouses of Dorset* (1970)

Cooksey, Alfred J.A. *Waggons and Coaches in Dorset* (1977)

Defoe, Daniel *A Tour Through the Whole of Great Britain* (1724)

Dolley, R.H.M. *Shaftesbury Hoard of Pence of Aethelraed II* (c. 1960)

Gerard, Thomas, *A Particular History of the Countie of Dorset* (c. 1625, published 1732 under the name of John Coker)

Hardy, Thomas, *Jude the Obscure* (1895)

Hopton, Frank, *Corruption & Reform: Municipal Government in the Borough of Shaftesbury 1730-1835* (1972)

Howarth, F. & J.A. Young, *A Brief History of the Water Supply of Shaftesbury, Dorset* (1972)

Hutchins, John, *The History and Antiquities of Dorset* (1st edition 1774 & 3rd edition 1863-1870)

Jervoise, E. FSA. *Shaftesbury, Dorset The Streets, Roads & Lanes* (1950)

Kaufman, C.M. *Romanesque Manuscripts* (1975)

Lawrence, Ian, *Fontmell Magna in Retrospect* (1988)

Leland, John, *Itinerary 1535-1543*

Light, Richard U. *Upjohn: A Study in Ancestry* (1990)

Long, F.C. *Tales of Old Shaftesbury* (1979)

Mayo, Charles, *Shastonian Records* (1889)
  The Minute Books of the Dorset Standing Committee 1646-50 (1902)

Newman J. & N. Pevsner *The Buildings of England Dorset* (1972)

Penn, K.J. *Historic Towns in Dorset* (1980)

Royal Commission on Historical Monuments *Historical Monuments in the County of Dorset Volume IV North* (1972)

Rutter, John *An Historical and Descriptive Account of the Town of Shaftesbury* unpublished manuscript of c. 1827
  History of the Shaftesbury Election 1830 (1826)
  Swyers vs. Rutter: A Plain Narration of Shastonian Occurrences without Comment (1826)

Rutter, William Farley *Shaftesbury 1890-1966: A Shastonian's Recollections* (1967)

Sydenham, Laura *Shaftesbury and Its Abbey* (1959)

Treves, Sir Frederick *Highways and Byways in Dorset* (1906)

Trustees of Shaftesbury School Chapel Arts Centre *Reminiscences of St. Rumbold's* (1988)

Victoria County History of Dorset

Dorset Record Society Vol. 12 *William Whiteway of Dorchester His Diary 1618-1635* (1991)

Wood, Michael *In Search of the Dark Ages* (1980)

Proceedings of the Dorset Natural History & Archaeological Society including:
  Vol 106 (1984) Cox, Margaret *Excavation within No. 8 Gold Hill*
  Vol 109 (1987) Draper, Jo *A Group of Early 19th Century Pottery from Shaftesbury, Dorset*
  Vol 110 (1988) Hopton, F.C. *The 1830 Parliamentary Election in Shaftesbury*

From Dorset County Museum library extracts from the Close, Liberate and patent Rolls of the 13th & 14th century.

Index